TRIUMPH HOUSE
Poetry with a Purpose

# *CHRISTIAN VERSE FROM THE UK*

Edited by

CHRIS WALTON

First published in Great Britain in 1998 by
TRIUMPH HOUSE
1-2 Wainman Road, Woodston,
Peterborough, PE2 7BU
Telephone (01733) 230749

HB ISBN 1 86161 283 4
SB ISBN 1 86161 288 5

# FOREWORD

Poetry is now becoming a more favoured way of expressing deep emotions and thoughts. This anthology contains over 180 authors - new and established alike - who put pen to paper to do just that.

*Christian Verse in the UK* is a lovingly crafted book of poetry and prose and many of the poems within tell a story or have a message that the writer would like to share. One thing the authors have in common is the love and faith they have in God.

With views from such a wide range of poets, this anthology is a 'must' for anyone in need of Christian inspiration.

Chris Walton
Editor

# CONTENTS

## DRINK OF ME

It is a hot day in the desert.
I'm dry and empty when I get to the well.
The stranger asks me for a drink.
He knows me.
He knows how empty I am.
The cool water refreshes me.
I am the dry vessel, now full and overflowing.
The pure water reveals my beautiful colour and patterns.
The light that showed my flaws and decay
Now magnifies the beauty my Creator formed.
His spirit has filled and cleansed me.
But oh, how quickly I empty and dry
How often I need to be refilled.

*Jacqueline Wentworth*


## BUILD ME A CHURCH

Build me a church,
Not of silver or gold,
But one that is filled,
With the young and the old.

Build me a church,
Where people can pray,
And leave me their burdens,
They have carried all day.

Build me a church,
Have it built in my name,
And you will be remembered,
When I return again.

*Edna Magill*

## TO HELP AND BE HELPED

When the world's at peace
That's when you find the essence of all you need
In a contented heart and settled mind
The best of yourself you will find

We're not made to be at constant strife
And battling against settlement in life
We have to learn to help each other
Only that way do we proceed further
God made us all different
That was part of his plan
But in exercising Christianity
We've to walk hand in hand
In all the things that can divide us up
Our human instinct can be touched by love
Everyone knows when someone treats them well
Because we've all known a little of the opposite
That's to say a living hell
Co-operation and understanding
Each individual's feelings and needs
Is the way to flourish
And cultivate our world from
God's precious seeds

So at the end of each day
Just pray
Clasp your hands and simply say
Thanks Lord for all who serve
Give them the help in life they deserve
We could not manage in life entirely alone

And so we reach
To love and respect each fellow person we meet
We remember how you told us of our neighbours
In the words that you preached
Don't ever let us feel too strong
That maybe we'll forget
That we need you too help us along
And in all our deeds
Let's be gracious with God's peace.

*Anne R Cooper*


## FLIGHT

Look, a line
Inscribed
On the underside
Of the sky
Fluffy with time:
Transitory.

Now, a line
Incised
- that would be
Something -
An opening within time
Over a waning sphere:

The space between
Described
By the heavy, slow
Moving trajectory
Of the solitary eagle
With his woeful cry.

*A Neal*

## THE SKY

The eye of the sky is a human thing,
Its raindrops the size of human tears;

The mouth of the sky is a human thing,
Its sounds uttered for human ears;

The ear of the sky is a human thing,
Its hearing a solace for human fears;

And the sky is mother to every tree,
Its oceans are filled with spirited clouds;

And the sky holds the blue of every sea,
And all the mountains its shadow shrouds;

And all the earth lifts its head to the sky,
Each little flower shows its preference!

And when God became man his human eyes
In the sky found Heaven's circumference!

*R D Ashby*


## BLESSED MOUNTAIN

The Mount of Beatitudes overlooking Galilee
A sea of distant calm and quiet repose,
Blessed mountain the lilies so profuse
Shine radiant now as always on thy hills,
This fragile flower with petals soft
An inspiration to us all of beauty and strength,
And when the flowers are spent and petals fall
Into the dust a million others shine and mushroom,
And so this same radiance grows in our hearts and minds
Not lost even when the last flush of red escapes us.

*Agnes McRae*

## Moffat Episcopal Church

Window, flowers, candle, all bathed in the sun -
The singing breaks out and the church has begun.
The flowers of the spirit are joy, hope and love,
So bless us and may we share flowers from above.

Window, flowers, candle - the light has moved on,
The service will finish and soon we'll be gone.
Christ bless us and help us amid the world's fight
And lead us and guide us, as candles shed light.

Window, flowers, candle - the sun gilds them all.
O God, save your children and answer our call,
Forget all our sins, and when this life is done
O threefold God, raise us to live in thy sun.

*Diana Richardson*


## The Sacrifice

T  he sacrifice given
H  eals our nation,
E  ncradled in his love, we receive his salvation.

S  uch mercy
A  nd unfathomable love
C  oupled with humility
R  eaches down to us.
I  ncomprehensible, that the King
F  orsakes his throne, compassion to bring.
I  f it were but one, if it were just you or me
C  hrist's undying love would still have reached to that tree.
E  verlasting, never failing, the loving sacrifice.

*Hazel Wright*

## BELIEVE OR KNOW?

If anyone had asked I would have replied, 'Yes I believe in God!'
I had proclaimed my belief in the Masonic ritual . . .
In the pub or drinking and arguing with friends I was able to state,
'Yes, I believe in God!'

I tried to live my life decently, being reasonably loyal,
truthful, and honest. I even went to church sometimes.
I was secure and comfortable in my belief,
smug in my associations and in my standing in the community.

When eventually my wife left me taking the children with her,
I was able to accept my change in circumstances with aplomb,
after all these things happen.
They left to live on another Hebridean island many miles away.

But despite my arrogance God believed in me.
There was the Bible I found stuffed down the back of the settee,
a paperback, modern version that had me fooled until I began to read it.
There was the verse of scripture that leaped out of a page,
*'So you believe in one God, so what, the devil also believes . . .'*
(1 James 2 :19) There was the Salvation Army man touting the
*'Warcry'* in the pub who spoke to me of whom I believed in,
there was the parish minister who preached on the verse,
there was the old lady that talked on that verse,
until at last I began to consider what it said.

The devil believes in God, the devil knows God exists
but the devil doe not know God in an intimate, real way.
I became determined to make my peace with God and
so travelled to my wife's home to attempt a reconciliation and
to share with her this good news, that we should and can know God,
not simply believe that He exists.

When I arrived my wife wouldn't let me speak
until she sat me down and to my amazement
produced a Bible I did not know she had.
'Listen,' she said, 'I have something to tell you,
I want you to look at this verse in Peter . . .'

*Jamie Hepburn*


## LIFE

Have you ever stopped to ponder - the reason why you're here?
Has it ever touched your mind - or do you really care?
Have you hid away in darkness - all thoughts of this today?
Or do you face the challenge - of what your life can say?

Unique among the billions - you could search but never find,
A mirror of yourself elsewhere - not just one of a kind,
Some might resemble a little - close to what you are,
But you will never find a perfect match - by travelling wide and far.

Imagine if your eye could see - mankind and that's quite a few,
But look inside this crowded world - there won't be another you,
No matter where you journey - no matter where you rest,
You'll always be your truly self - you'll never fail that test.

Life is but a passing vapour - a few faded words on a page,
It's over before you know it - those years take on your age,
Don't let your heart be troubled - the grave is not the end,
For that is when we really need - a loving, caring friend.

Your body is but just a shell - to last you for a while,
Ensure that you have arranged - your name placed in God's file,
For He is your creator - on you He breathes His smile,
Live cautiously and faithful - make sure He's got your time.

*Brian McSweeney*

## AN EASTER PRAYER

Come Holy Spirit cleanse my soul, and break the bonds
of sin and fear,
Take from me Lord the fear of death, that I may look
on your face most dear,
Be with me Lord, O Holy One,
forgive the sins that I have done,
Give me your Grace, give me your Love,
that only comes from Heaven above.
O hear me Lord in your blessed way,
oh guide me Jesus, day by day,
that in the ever shining Light I may walk
in your priceless sight,
With Holy peace, assurance too,
that I'll be ever near to you,
That I may humbly bend the knee, to you who
triumphed at Calvary,
And at the end of life's long race, at last I'll see
the blessed face,
Of my Lord, and Saviour, and my Friend,
Who lives in Heaven, in time without end.

*R McCurdy*


## FAITH

Faith is the guide that holds our hand
To guard us through life's alien land
A star to lead us on aright
When trouble turns our day and night.

Faith is a vision, sharp and clear,
That brings God's promises more near.
Faith is a secret, sweetly sealed,
Like treasure hidden in a field.

A joyful secret, carefree, gay.
Our cloudy pillar for the day,
And fire by night to light the ground,
And spread a glory all around.

Faith is a shield and shelter warm,
A covert from the rain and storm,
A mystic pledge of sins forgiven,
A shining ladder up to heaven.

*C M Hanson*

## ON FINDING GOD

I have learned to love Thee all too late
  Oh Beauty so ancient and yet so new.
    You were within me all the while,
    But I searched out the pomp and style
  That is this world. It seems now true:
I should have scanned my inner state.

You were already with my soul
  While I, disfigured like, would fall among
    The lovely, outward workings of Your hands.
    But all these things about, if seas or lands,
  Would never be except they had their song
In Thee. You make them whole.

You called. You cried aloud to me.
  You broke those walls which bar the light.
    You shone. Your smell enveloped all
    That is me. I am now small.
  But for another touch and taste of Thee I fight.
I am inflamed. Your face I long to see.

*A R Baird*

## EXCUSE ME, I THINK THERE HAS BEEN A MISTAKE

There appears to be an error
A terrible mistake has been made
I thought I was going to heaven
But in hell I seem to be laid

I expected to see the angels
In bright clothing and radiant light
But I'm surrounded by demon-like creatures
A frightening and hideous sight

I don't understand what has happened
I lead a pretty good life
Was kind to my friends and neighbours
Worked hard for my children and wife

I went to church the odd Sunday
Gave cash to the 'Children in Need'
Helped run the Sunday School outing
Showed an example to all by my deeds

I believe I see an old colleague
A religious fanatic I recall
Forever talking of Jesus
And advising repentance by all

I've tried my best to reach him
But a chasm is barring my way
There seems to be no crossing
So here it appears I must stay

He appears at peace and contented
With similar folks by his side
While I am frightened and lonely
With no others near me or in sight

Now he sits down at a banquet
With a figure who shines like the sun
While my surroundings get darker
And screams and torment make me numb

I wish I could return and warn others
Of the horrors and impending fate
For those who reject the Lord Jesus
And leave thoughts of our God till too late.

*Ron Beaton*


## THIS TREE

This tree has seen my children grow from young boys into men.
It heard their laughter, dried their tears
and sheltered them through all the years,
when like young trees they'd bend and sway
with every breeze that passed their way.

It heard their cries of pure delight
on Hallowe'en and bonfire night
and shared their joy on Christmas Eve
with gifts to give and to receive.

From youth to man so straight and strong
knowing the line twixt right and wrong.
Then came the day, they flew the nest
and tried their wings and passed the test.

Now tree and I watch from afar
amazed at just how wise they are
and I reach out and touch this tree
which through the years has sheltered me.

*Carol Ann Mason*

## A PRAYER

Not wealth, nor fame
I pray for Thee, O God!
But graces to share
Your wisdom and love.
Not joys, not gains
Do I ask Thee O Lord!
But a heart who loves
And a faith to endure.
It is not the world
I seek from Above
But a soul who is pure
Where Heaven is the treasure.

*Nell Hynard*

## BROTHER AGAINST BROTHER

Let us lay aside our weapons,
Those cruel words that hurt and maim.
Grenade and machine gun are nothing
To the power of the tongue.

We are all brothers and sisters,
Bought and redeemed and loved.
May that peace that passes all understanding bind us,
For we are no great lights on our own.

We should pray for the Spirit's healing power
Even though a gulf divides us now.
One day we will not know pain or pride,
But in heaven we shall know everlasting peace.

*David Tallach*

## TIME

Since time immemorial, man has been borne along almost
imperceptibly by time, governed by time,
in effect under subjection to time,
our lives constantly controlled and revolving incessantly
in and around time as it inexorably grinds on.

It is a stupendous fact that time, incapable in itself,
and needless of having any contact with,
or physically touching any aspect of the universe,
nevertheless, quietly, insidiously takes its toll on everything
encapsulated in creation, effectively and noticeably creating change
and decay with its passage.

How incalculably precious is our allotted time,
the time given us to compare how short indeed it is,
in comparison with the great eternity looming before us
where time will be suspended forever.
We are continually faced with the awesome reality which we must
comprehend - that is, in time each day given us
is also a day taken from us and here we have the amazing
phenomenon of the subtraction of time by addition of time.

Time is employed by the eternity beckoning us on to its brink.
Our time in time is not our own time.
God is giving us time to seek for Christ in time.
It is imperative that we use this time now, and that we do so before
eternity claims us, because then, the time for opportunities
will have gone, time for prayers will vanish, time for gospel invitations
will be lost forever, and should we not be in Christ in time
we shall be utterly forlorn and desolate as we draw our last breath
in *time* and step into the great unknown . . .

Make time, in time, to be in time, for time and *eternity*.

*M MacDonald*

## LITTLE OLD LADY

A little lady old and grey
Ninety years young passed away
She used to toddle down the street
For her pension once a week
Then go off to the butchers
For her little joint of meat.

You would always see her waving
When anyone went by
And sometimes at the window
You often saw her cry.

She had a nice big tabby cat
It was her pride and joy
She called him little Charlie
It was her little boy.

She wasn't very modern
Just oil lamps for a light
And a tap was in the garden
Which she covered every night.

She always had a glass of stout
Sometimes a tot of gin
Then go up to the window
And then she'd start to sing.

She never had much money
And just sitting in her chair
You would often see her knitting
And say a little prayer.

You would always see her bake her bread
And sometimes currant buns
She never had a family
Not a daughter or a son.

Now if ever you go that way
You know she won't be there
Waving at the window
Just say a little prayer.

*B Salter*


## STAR OF BETHLEHEM

A star shines bright, in the sky tonight.
A star of silver, shining down its light.
This is the one, the most pure of all.
While all the other stars, appear so small.

This is the star, most holy in the sky.
Shining so bright, it blinds the eye.
The 'Star of Bethlehem,' that's its name.
The Son of God, was born under its flame.

The Bethlehem star, guided those men so wise.
Beheld the Son, before their very eyes
Frankincense, gold and myrrh, gifts were given.
To the Son of God, who came from heaven.

The Son of God, born in a stable so bare.
The animals so lowly, were also there.
Life began that day, the day Jesus was born.
Animals in the stable, kept this holy child warm.

In your hours of loneliness, gaze to the sky above.
The 'Star of Bethlehem' represents a pure love.
Stars in the sky above, will forever shine.
The 'Star of Bethlehem' will shine, till the end of time.

*Kevin P Collins*

## ANSWER TO PRAYER

Amelia Jane walked up the long shingled path,
savouring the fact that today she was on her own.
On Sundays she attended this church with her older sister Gillian
and several of her school friends
but today she was intent on having an adventure all on her own.
Pushing open the heavy oak door she entered the beautiful old building
enjoying the cool and peaceful atmosphere,
afternoon sunlight streamed through the stained glass windows
and sun dust danced down the beams of light.
Walking on tip-toe she came to the pew that her parents usually sat in,
should she kneel here she wondered or dare she go up
to the high alter and kneel in front of the cross.
Amelia Jane had been told in Sunday School that God listens
to all our prayers no matter where we are
but she felt closer to Him nearer the cross.
The church was very quiet save for the heavy rhythmic thud
sounding from the vestry, this was from the church clock
and not at all scary.
Amelia knew the vestry well as occasionally
she had been chosen to ring the bell for Sunday School,
this bell worked on a pulley system not at all like the six bells
that were high up in the belfry.
Amelia had never climbed the stairs up to the ringers
but had often gazed up at her Aunt and Uncle who were
members of the Ringers' Band.
Also in the vestry were the choir members' robes
and these were a real attraction, Amelia longed to be a member
of the choir but had been told because she would never keep still,
she was a fidget she would be a distraction to the other children.
Poor Amelia Jane she longed to sing and make a joyful noise
as the minister had said in his sermon last Sunday,
this was the reason for Amelia's lone visit,
she was going to ask God to let her sing to him and naturally
to wear those beautiful long choir robes.

Kneeling, Amelia put her hands together and pointed
her fingers upwards as if to wing her prayer right up to heaven.
Her prayer was short but sounded so poignant in its simplicity.
'Oh God I do so want to sing to you and make a joyful noise
and the Minister has said that anything we ask in Jesus' name
you will grant us, so thanks a lot,
Amen and love from Amelia Jane!'
Little did Amelia know that the old verger had been
a silent witness to all that had gone on and the faith
of this little child had touched his heart.
After Amelia had left the church he set off to see the Minister,
and, yes, Amelia was allowed to join the choir that very
next Sunday and no voice rang out more cheerfully than hers!

*Jennifer Ashman*


## UNTITLED

Alone I sit and wonder
What does life really mean.
Success at work, money to spend
or achieving our greatest dream
We're all searching for improvement
to reach us to the top,
No time to look around us
but for a moment *stop.*
Achieving all in this world will
not make us complete,
Unhappiness is not far away
there's always room to weep.
There's a verse in *St Mark's Gospel*
that my thoughts fit like a mould.
'What profit a man if he gains the world
        but then to lose his soul?'

*Noleen Leyburn*

## THE END AND THE BEGINNING

Am confined to bed, I have got the flu
Feeling so ill, I have just turned ninety-two
Am in a home, where there is care
But love and compassion, are very rare.

Have lost all my teeth, nothing works underneath
Need spoon-fed, need to be led
Such an old nuisance, keep wetting the bed.
Eyes getting dim, they say going blind
One thing is sure, am still of sound mind.

Always giving, I know, loud moans and deep groans
What can be done, with this old string of bones?
No-one to talk to, no-one to hear
No-one has time, to come anywhere near
A comforting hug, a kind loving touch
Costs nothing at all, but can mean so much.

Close my eyes tightly, think of my life
My handsome son, my own darling wife
All are now gone - I have no kin at all
No living relative, whom I can recall.

Yes - I have my strong faith in the Lord
He is my Saviour, my Support, and my Rod
He raises me up when feelings are sad
And fills this old crock, with tidings so glad.

Lord, pray take me soon,
From this wrinkled old shell, up to your heavenly home to dwell
I have no earthly fear of death's dark door
I know I will live, in your house ever more.

And there I shall meet,
All my loved ones of old
At the feet of my Jesus
Our arms shall enfold.

*Vina Lack*


## TO A TREE

To a tree they nailed you,
to a tree.
A living thing, now dead,
but destined
for eternity.

A tree cut down in the prime
of life.
While the sap
was still flowing,
strong and true.

Fashioned it roughly,
no craftsmanship here.
Not worked on lovingly
as you would have done,
on your carpenter's workbench.

This tree, used so brutally
for a gruesome task -
what immortality!

A cross of wood
misunderstood,
split by nails
and soiled with blood,
spilt for me.

*Maggie Smith*

# GOD IS *IT*

Once I was asked by a child of seven,
'What's God doing up in Heaven? The world's falling apart!'
What a question! Where do I start?
My answer, thank God came, from the heart.

'When I think of God, I think of *It*.'

'*It?*'

'Spring flowers and April showers;
Night-time dreams of your favourite ice cream;
Poisonous snakes and chocolate cheesecakes;
They are all part of *It*.'

'God is cheesecake? God is *It?* What does that mean?'

*It* is everything that ever was and ever will be.
*It* is life everlasting, which is a very long time. *It* goes up and down,
                                                        on and on,
Like a free roller coaster ride. Imagine a roller coaster, the ride of
                                                        your life -
And there's no getting off.'

'I like roller coasters!' she screamed. 'it sounds like fun!
But if I'm *It*, if I'm God, why don't I know *It?*'

'At school you learn how to add and subtract
Life is a school where you learn certain facts
You learn to be kind, to give and to take
You grow and learn by mistake.'

'But if we are all *It*,' she rightfully asked, 'why are people
                                                        starving to death?
Why do people kill each other?'

(Where has the innocence of childhood gone?)

'We all make choices on what we create. We make mistakes one by one
And blame it on
Fate.
But soon we will learn just who we are.
Soon we'll wake up to the fact we're Divine stars.'

'Oh, what can I do to help *It* improve?
What can *I* do?'

'You can help make *It* great because you are *It*.
The key is love, Love is that's what *It's* all about,
But don't tell Brian Bradley -
He might try to kiss you!'

'Ugh!'

Don't you just love *It?*

**Michael Wycks**


## PEOPLE

There are areas of deprivation,
Which saps the strength of the population.
In this time of equality, partnership and participation
Why are there so many divisions of the nation?
Many are isolated by social exclusion
Is there anyone out there who's found a solution?
There's no money for this,
And no money for that
Yet, sometimes money can be found at the drop of a hat!
Caring, consideration, compassion are words we hear bandied about,
What people would like to see is this carried out.
Let your conscience be your guiding light
If ever in doubt about what is right.

**Margaret Meek**

## THE MASTERPIECE

Look at us!
Flotsam and jetsam,
Thrown up by the tides of life.
Battered, pierced, broken,
Bleached by use and time.
Once useful, treasured possessions,
Some now discarded to one side,
Others lost through carelessness or neglect,
But all - all ignorant of purpose,
Of where we're going next.

But then he comes.
The Beachcomber,
Searching for treasures,
Meeting his needs.
He stops, a glint in his eye,
Picks up, dusts down
And carries caringly home
All that he desires.
No longer refuse or redundant parts,
The items gathered take on meaning now:
Potential sources of beauty,
The missing jewels in his crown.

And as each part is placed
Alongside all the rest,
The Artist builds his picture
Until not one is left
Unused, untouched, neglected by his hand.
He needs each one to finish his great work.
A single part removed would spoil the Craftsman's plan.

Until . . . now look!
What once would grieve the eyes
Is changed, renewed,
Arranged in harmony.
Disparate, lonely parts unite,
Together blend and cause delight.
The Artist's work revealed his heart.
A work of love. A work of art.

*Gillian Lang*


## ETERNITY

Are you afraid of what's to come,
Can you meet your fate,
For it belongs to everyone,
Will you pass through the gate?

Have you been true to your inner self,
Lived your life, as best you can,
Not perfect, no one ever is,
A title, not claimed even by the 'Son'
Who came to us, to be a Man.

When the call to leave the world arrives,
Go, with the knowledge the soul survives,
Place yourself, in the arms of him
Who will cleanse your mind, and heart, of sin.

The step aloft, to the promised land,
A land where times stands still, and your loved ones
Wait to take your hand, never to part again.

When you promised to love forever,
And one of you went ahead, that love never died,
It is with you still, so go, be with him again,
Live until the end of time, for that is Eternity.

*Laura Creed*

## THROUGH THE NIGHT

Lord, I know you are listening
At this late hour.
I know you can answer,
I know of your power.

I struggle for sleep
But sleep will not come
Shadows surround me,
Rest, I find none.

The house is still and quiet
With gentle sounds of sleeping
Can anyone hear
As I lie silently weeping?

Pain is my companion
With me again,
Exhaustion overwhelming
But who is my friend?

The whole world sleeps
Yet I am awake.
Please send me a friend, God,
Or my heart it will break.

Yet, in the dark silence
There glimmers a light
A light getting brighter
As it shines through the night.

'My child, what you're asking
You have in your hands.
Now lean on me harder
In order to stand.

I'll reach out and hold you,
As I stand by your side
A friend that knows all
Of your fears near and wide.

No need to pretend
Or try to explain
All thoughts deep inside you
I already see plain.

So, come and lie down,
And rest in me now.
The silence becomes peace
As we prayerfully bow.'

*Kay McKee*


## HANDS

Your hands are
precious to me,
of supple shape
and good to see,
they soothe and stroke
with tender touch,

hold me close
when I'm afraid
and in good fellowship,
swinging along
with striding step
in rare winter sunshine.

they bring refreshment,
open doors and
often times through
all the day,
and in the night,
hand clasps hand
just for the grace.

*Monica Redhead*

# CHILDHOOD RECOLLECTIONS

Soft whisper of surprises long dreamed
Sounds brought to life by moving my feet
Rays of pale moonlight straight beamed
Guiding my eyes as I peep.

Surely night's curtain should be drawn
For all to see the wonders of this day
Oh so delayed arrival of the dawn
Each hour in sleep one less in which to play.

At last a movement in the house
I thought they'd sleep away the morning
My careful plans just made to rouse
Abandoned with my mother's calling.

An excited search through a stocking well filled
Of a Christmas tree laden a glimpse too hurried
A breakfast of sizzling bacon well grilled
Prepared by my mother as ever unflurried.

Cold streets with paving stones white with frost
Church bells stirring the air with their peals
Hurrying, scurrying, no time to be lost
Staccato echo of mother's high heels.

The crib in the corner, a wondrous sight
A warm glow of candles on altar high
Gentle red wink of the sanctuary light
Congregation hushed as the priest draws nigh.

I keep my head bowed and my prayers I say
Yet my thoughts start to wander then settle on toys
With a fort and soldiers long promised I play
My head filled with dreams known only to boys.

The Mass is so long and I've said all my prayers
My knees start to ache I'm sure they will crack
With each little fidget my father he glares
A fat girl with pigtails keeps prodding my back.

With he priest's blessing the end comes at last
Through the last carol I'm filled with dismay
My chance to say thank you has almost slipped past
Oh I do thank you God for the joy of this day.

*Ray Cliffe*

## SEARCHING

Lost, alone and frightened
Needing a place to be
Needing a certain somebody
To be there for me.

Holding on to dreams
That seldom come true
Where to turn for hope
For tomorrow to start anew.

Searching ever endlessly
Till I found You there
It took a while for me to learn
I'd find You there in prayer.

Now silently together
I tell You all I am
The freedom You have given me
The ability to understand.

Lost, alone and frightened
Needing a place to be
In prayer I found you Father
And You were there for me.

*Debbie Finkel*

## GOOD FRIDAY AND BEYOND

Look to the Tree -
The carpenter made a cross of wood -
Did He see
His life given away
For you and me?
Look to the Cross -
A cruel death,
Man cries out with pain!
Darkness all over the world,
Would we see the dawn again?
Then out of the darkness
Came His wonderful light!
The new Day burst forth,
Sunlight out of night!
Earth and Heaven rejoiced.
Angel voices rang across the sky!
Look to the Cross
And lift it high -
An everlasting symbol of His Glory!

*Elizabeth Egerton*


## PRAYER FOR FORGIVENESS

Lord, I do not praise your name,
Though the joys and blessings come.
All too easily I forget
To give thanks to the Holy One.

Self is a vain, blind dog
Who struts and is always alone.
Never seeing the needs of others
Feeding pride with every moan.

As autumn turns to winter
So many things get in the way.
The doubts and fears grow
And then I kneel to pray.

Let me learn from my mistakes
And rise like the dove.
Lord, light up my darkness
By your grace and love.

*Maureen Macnaughtan*


## REMEMBER THE WATCHFUL PROTECTOR

When within the dark cloud of emptiness descends
and the path ahead seems fraught with unending strain
remember the watchful protector.
When every effort seems constantly aborted
and confidence slips into a dismal sag, unco-ordinate
remember the watchful protector.
When everyone's back speaks of cold refusal
and no-one understands, though advice flows as usual
Remember the watchful protector.
When order gives way to disorder
and significance to impotent insignificance
remember the watchful protector.
When fear, crushed beneath the words of judgement
cannot find the unconditional embrace
remember the watchful protector.
When you in your heart seek only to open
to face what you must and make a new start
then here you will find, the caring eye of love
the watchful protector, remembered at last.

*Marion Elvera*

## WRITTEN IN CARLISLE CATHEDRAL

Lord, in the silence of this place
    I look above,
All the peace I find herein
    I take with love.
I yield myself unto thy holy will -
    I am thine own,
Take me and mould me from this day
    For thine alone.

*Mary Crabtree*


## THE WORD

The Word,
Once spoken,
Sending ripples out through all time and space.
Filling the Universe with a cacophony of sound.
Giving glory to the one,
Who spoke,
The Word.

*Jennie Hall*


## BATTLE OF HOPE

As I walk through the land of the dead
I am smitten and accused by those who
Hate me. For I am with the living. My
Soul doth cry out to God 'Joshua' yes
Even He, who they did hate before me,
Yet He did rise above all, yea, even
Death, unto eternity.

*Edward Lee Crosby*

## I MET JESUS

I met Jesus in the hillside,
As I walked the paths of green.
I feel His presence all around me -
Though He wasn't to be seen.
I heard the streams as they trickled by,
Singing gently on the way,
I heard the birds as they praised my Lord
As they always do each day.
The flowers gently turned their faces
To face the summer sun,
Butterflies settled on the purple buddleja,
And bees on the thistle, one by one.
The pheasants called and chattered
Near the river bank.
Beauty and creation all around me
For which Jesus I had to thank.
His peace was there, like a blanket
Gently covering me.
I wanted to stay there for ever.
Nowhere else I wanted to be.
This peace we want wherever we are
In the bustle of life each day.
Surrounding us in everything,
Our work, all sadness and all play.
So as I walked that hillside
From cares and worries, so free,
I asked God to let me take that peace
Everywhere with me.

*June Bootle*

## To Be?

What was Maria to do? She'd asked her priest about it.
'You can't do anything, Maria - it would be a *mortal sin.*'
So she asked the doctor.
'To get rid of the child would be against nature . . .
I can't help you my dear, *have* the child, then hope for the best.'
He watched Maria as she slowly made her way from his door,
'Poor, poor woman, four children already.
The first one blind, the second dead, the third deaf-and-dumb,
Then he thought of the last one with tuberculosis like Maria herself.
What was worse, her husband had contracted syphilis . . .
Surely, the new child shouldn't be born . . . reason forbade it.'
Johann, her husband, was carried home by two men both as drunk
as *he* was, it was already the next morning.
This was by no means unusual either. On his way to work,
late of course, he shouted to Maria, 'We can't have it, Woman . . .
It'll be born deaf, crippled, or even blind!'
She remembered what a close friend of hers had said to her before
their wedding.
'Johann's wage-earning capacity will decline with his inability
to keep sober!' Then she thought of the day - in April last -
when they'd made love briefly one morning, before she'd
been fully awake.
Maria then remembered their first meeting.
She'd been cleaning the church floor. Maria had heard him singing
as he came through the large oak doors.
He seemed so handsome then. He'd stopped singing, then had quietly
spoken to her; she remembered how she'd trembled, dropped the
floor cloth, then spilled water over his boot. Johann hadn't sworn
at her *that* day.
As the months passed they seemed to get used to the idea of another
mouth to feed. On the 16th of December a boy was born to them both.
All her husband could say was: 'Isn't he ugly? . . . his ears are big too.'
She noticed that the baby had a strong cry, at least that
was something.

Maria asked Johann what they should call their son.
'Name him after the dead one!' he answered unlovingly.
So, arrangements for the baptism of their boy Ludwig were made
for the next day by his mother, Maria Magdalena Beethoven.

*Richard Stoker*


## EASTER (SPRING)

Rotting wood where once it stood.
Darkening sky, grey and misted over,
Frost, cold nights and piercing wind.
Despair, gloom and stiffening limb.
Weeping, crying and failing breath.
Three crosses standing on a lonely hill
A mother weeping at the foot of rugged timber.
'It is finished' the cry - this is death.

But then the time of joy and laughter.
Bursting buds and bleating lambs.
Bluebells peeping in a wooded glade,
The gardener taking from his shed his spade
Laid resting through those gloomy days
When all seemed lost.
Bursting blossom round the tomb,
Changing each day by new buds and leaves
Anxious to display their unique charm to all the world.

The Stone is rolled away, only garments lay,
Where He who died for all was put to rest.
Then new life has come 'He is risen',
Bursting forth His love into the world like spring.
Anxious for all mankind to know. His love is here for them.
A light shining into the dark crevices of His world
Where sin and decay, do not welcome this stone that's rolled away,
Never to be returned - He lives for all.

*Geoffrey Ackroyd*

## IT MATTERS

It matters how we live each day,
The things we do, the words we say.
When we awake and say our prayers
We know He's there and that He cares.
We try to live our lives for Him
Although we battle with our sin.
The Bible is our daily bread -
We need to read it to be fed.
Then our faith in Him will grow
And fruits of the spirit begin to show.
It matters how we live each day
The things we do - the words we say.

Our lives should show the Saviour's love
Reflecting His beauty from above.
O teach us Lord, rebuke us too
As we strive each day to be like You.
It's not an easy road we tread
We need to heed the words You said -
'Resist the devil and he will flee
And you will have the victory'
Yes it matters how we live each day,
The things we do, the words we say.

Remember these words and try to be
A shining light that all may see
Jesus our Saviour shining through
So they will want to know Him too.
Holy spirit use us and fill
So we may be able to do Your will,
Forgive our sins Lord, teach us anew
How we should live our lives for You.
For it *matters* how we live each day
It *matters* what we do and say.

*K Simpson*

# THE TREE

Torn by the storm
the great tree stood mute awaiting attention
and we were sad
for we had loved that tree in all its changing moods.

We heard the chainsaw whirr
and, breath-bated, wept for the stricken giant.
All day we watched, compelled to view its fate.

But we were wrong - the end was not to be -
God and the tree-surgeon knew better.
In their wise hands the tree was shaped anew
to stand once more head high against the sky.
Stunted, it seemed lopsided to our gaze
and we slow to trust in God or man
could not envisage what might be, saying
'It will never be the same.'

Now, eighteen months beyond that dreadful day,
I gaze with wonder on the shimmering giant.
The evening sun shines silver on its leaves
as, clothed again, more beauteous than before,
the new-shaped branches stretch towards the heavens.

Rent by life's gales
the stricken soul stands like our tree before its Maker,
surrendering to its fate
and He with strong but patient hands reshapes us
oft against our will.
We cannot know the outcome only watch and wait
trusting that He knows best
and in the end
what unexpected glory may be born
out of the shattered remnants of our strength.

*Elaine Lawrence*

## SPRING AND SUMMER

The clatter of clogs in the early morn.
The winters cold and covering white.
As I shuffle to work in the early light
The thoughts of toil that is waiting me.
The day ahead and it must be said
I hate the dirt, the noise, which I dread
That I endure for my daily bread.
I dream the passing of present time
And yearn for the future season.
My earth, my grass, my flowers.
My garden is the reason.

*A Harrison*


## SEA OF FORGIVENESS

There's a shrouded sea of forgiveness
Within our God's own land,
Where all sins are laid to rest
When cast there by His hand.

That sea remains unfathomably deep:
No mortal man may know
How high the waves above it leap,
How low its waters flow.

The Lord Himself draws no net
Nor hoists a sail thereon,
For He pleases to forgive
Repentant sinners' wrongs.

O that we human beings could
Have such a sea within,
Where His forgiveness ever would
Drown the guilt of sin.

*Sharon Marie Johnston*

## SOLDIERS OF CHRIST

Do not mourn for things that cannot be,
Turn your thoughts to Christ's sacrifice on Calvary,
As Christ did, do the same,
Shoulder your cross, march bravely on,
We are all soldiers in Christ.

Our backs may be bowed, with the pressures we face,
But we march knowing we're wrapped in God's grace.
Follow his footsteps, where he leads, follow,
Be not one to wallow in grief,
Talk to your saviour, gain your relief.

Turn to face each new day,
Bend your knees and pray.
Be not ashamed, pick up your cross,
Follow your saviour, he'll show you the way,
We are all soldiers in Christ.

*Jane Dyson*


## THE HILL

In the crowded room I longed for solitude;
A chance to pray and learn from God.
People all around me blocked the silence -
My heart raged and longed for stillness.

High up in the hills I wandered
Searching for the Spirit I knew lived there;
I looked down into the crowded room
And saw the Spirit resting on each head.
In the midst of many sang the Spirit
Conjured into life by love and joy.

Humbled, I returned to sit among my neighbours
And opened up my heart to love.

*Althea Hayton*

## A CHILD IN CHRIST

We've all been little children
So weak and apt to stray
Let our parents take control of us
To put us in the Saviour's Way.

He took the little children
And blessed them everyone
He lifted them up into His arms
For He was His Father's Son.

He said unto the people
'Suffer the children to come to Me
Be as humble as one of these
And the Kingdom of Heaven you'll see.

So children love your parents
As Jesus loves you so
They'll guide you on the right path
Wherever you may go.

Dear little children love your Saviour
On the Cross on which He died
For He has risen from His grave
And in Heaven He does reside.

Sitting at the Heavenly throne
Do trust him with your heart
And when your life is over
With him you will never part.

*Ivor Wilson*

## PRAYER POWER

Call upon me, said the Lord, and I will answer you,
For is anything too difficult for me to do? -
Able to do exceeding abundantly above all we think or ask,
For with God there's no such thing as an impossible task.
And being fully absolved from the wrong we have done
Through the precious blood of His beloved Son,
To the throne of grace we may boldly draw near,
In full assurance of faith, without hindrance or fear,
To humbly ask forgiveness wherein we've gone astray,
Knowing the blood of Jesus can cleanse every sin away;
To ascribe heartfelt praise for God's loving kindness shown
And to make our every need to the Father of mercies known.
For God's ears are ever open to His people's prayers,
As he bids us upon Him to cast all our cares,
Promising to draw near when to Him we draw nigh
And to bear our burdens when upon Him we rely.
For Jesus said, 'Ask, and you shall receive,'
That your joy may be full, when we steadfastly believe
That God will answer, in faith that cannot be stirred,
Fully persuaded He will honour every promise in His word;
And when His wise counsel we daily heed and obey,
With all known sin in our lives confessed and put away;
And when we're at one with our brother, and with our families,
Praying in the light of God's word, and not selfishly.
For this is our confidence, when we pray in His will,
He will assuredly hear, and our petitions fulfil.
This vital part of the Christian armour, let us therefore use aright,
Remembering, when on our knees, we are men and women of might,
As the fervent prayers of the righteous much shall avail,
For when we pray in Christ's name, we are sure to prevail.

*Ian Caughey*

## POLISH CHRISTMAS EVE

The gentle rustle of coconut palms,
The surge of white on the coral boom,
And two lone figures on the empty shore
Scanning above the navy blue dome.

From the land of the Black Madonna they come,
A wintry country far away,
From Czestechowa, the holy shrine,
Where suppliant pilgrims make their way.

A hand points out the first glittering star
On the eve when the Virgin's son was to be,
To rejoint the bond between God and man,
The long-lost solidarity.

They return and invite me to their tent
Where a table is set, with one empty place,
Left for the stranger who will come.
Would I join them, please, and fill the space?

Here in this southern continent
Should the crib figures always be white?
For a black Madonna and child would be
At a point where all the world can unite.

*John Jenkin*


## GOD'S LOVE FOR MAN

Jesus His life for man did give
So that in Him and His presence we can live
He wants to dwell in our heart
To be Lord of all not just apart.

Jesus wants us to have fellowship with Him every day
His love and grace to experience unconditionally
We must walk with Jesus close to our side
So that He can be our guide.

We should listen and obey His still small voice
And in His love and goodness rejoice
Everyday, this one thing we must do
Spend time alone with God in prayer and not forget to listen too.

If we want Jesus in others to see
We must be willing to Jesus bow the knee
Only then will people see Jesus does live
And if we come to Him, new life He will give.

*William Moore*


# IN THE MORNING

Her child-wide eyes filled with drops of warm, silvery water.
Slowly the jewels over-brimmed
and the delicate pools trickled a stream down, across the ivory cheeks
and splashed onto her dress.

Soon rivulets were pouring down, down, splashing down and
dripping onto her mourning clothes,
and urgent sobs shook her fragile frame, growing to such a force
that her whole body shook.

She prayed, 'Oh, God, where is He?'

'Mary. Oh Mary.'

The frightened child listened, she strained her ears, but nothing heard
save the birds.
She turned her aching head and nothing saw save the gardener,
silhouetted in the sun.

'Mary. Oh, Mary.'

And little Mary Magdalen believed.

*Sue J Eaton*

## QUIET TIMES

A quiet time's essential
For all of us each day,
A time to pause and ponder
A time for us to pray.

To recoil for a moment
From the pace of life, and see
How oft the picture changes
When we find tranquillity.

Problems insurmountable
We find may now be solved,
Thing which seemed so intricate
Become much less involved.

Our Lord would often take Himself
Away from all the crowd,
For the still small voice is stronger
Than the voice that's always loud.

In the quiet of the hills
There is so much to be found,
For nature speaks in many tongues
And her teachings are profound.

So try to seek some quiet times
Each and every day,
It may be that the Master
Has some special thing to say.

*John Osborne*

## MEMORIES OF HOME

Memories cling around me
Of our little house and home.
Of the little old-world garden,
And the fields we used to roam.

The roses red beside the door,
The daisies on the lawn,
The rambling roses by the wall
Now all of these are gone.

The little burn still ripples on
Where we often played
The trees we climbed or sat around
Under their leafy shade.

The meadow bright with buttercups
And lovely flowers so gay,
In memory I see them still
And smell the new-mown hay.

Our lovely home has gone now,
And flowers bloom no more,
Nothing left but memories
Of the roses round the door.

Many dear friends have passed away
I remember them with love,
But know that we shall meet again
In our lovely home above.

*Maud Nicholl*

## UNQUESTIONABLE PR

I remember when I was a small
Child, in the school assembly hall
Fearfully listening to the old, wrinkled
And bald-headed priest, his white eyebrows
And tufty white ear-brows; he
Stood at the head of the school,
Yet despite his age; he was demonically tall.

He ordered us to be good,
Or God would send a flood
Like he'd done before. His
Words rattled through my head
The fear took its hold
His weekly doctrine
Subdued my mind; it became as clear as mud.

Now in my adult years, I follow
That teaching like a hollow
Zombie, with no brain in my head.
I'm like the blind man who follows
His dog, but he can feel his guide
I must trust the words of a scary
Old priest; and pray it doesn't bring me sorrow.

*David Webster*

## THE INSTIGATOR

Quietly He came,
Slipping into the world
Unnoticed - the perfect guise,
A sleeping agent.

A little flurry - yes,
A tale of supernatural sights,
But told by superstitious men
And foreign sorcerers.

Not enough, you would think,
To change the course of history.
But thirty years of preparation
Following centuries of expectation

Needed barely three years of action
To light an inextinguishable fuse
Now smouldering down the centuries.
When can we expect the bang?

*S Mourant*


## INSIGHT

I managed to read
But I did not learn.
I strained to listen
But I did not hear.
I tried to look
But I did not see.

Now that I have read
And learned,
I listened and heard,
I looked and saw.

Only now can I read
To learn,
Listen to hear and
Look to see.

*'Do you not know? Have you not heard?*
*Has it not been told you from the beginning?*
*Have you not understood since the earth was founded?'*
                                            *Isaiah 40:21*

*Jenny Lim*

## A MOTHER'S LOVE - A MEDITATION FOR EASTER

Crowded on every side
and yet lost and alone
in her tormented thoughts and misery
How could it end like this?

She could not even bear to look at her own
for fear that her heart would break
Through a blur of tears
she could see his face etched in pain
as they hauled him up on the cross
that would crucify him.

The taunts and mocking deafened
the cries of those who loved him
'Aren't you the Christ? Save yourself and us!' they yelled.

It was at that moment, her thoughts returned
to a day long ago
when her heart had been jubilant
at the news of his birth.
She recalled the words of the angel
that she was highly favoured;
and would give birth to the Holy One,
the Son of God.

How she had wondered what those words meant
and how it could possibly be.
She had treasured the good news
that a saviour would be born
and that he was the Christ.

She had marvelled too as Simeon had exclaimed
that he had seen God's salvation,
and yet hadn't he also foretold that
'A sword will pierce your own soul too.'

She hadn't realised until that moment
the cost of being blessed by God.
Yet what an honour
to bear and to bring up the Lord of all
the Creator, King and Redeemer of the world.
She could only bow in adoration
at his holiness.

*Karen Spracklen*

## FOR GOOD FRIDAY - A WOMAN OF BETHLEHEM

'Before me is the man that I have hated for over thirty years. The hatred
has filled my waking moments and my dreams. For all those years my
life has been filled with bitterness and sorrow, with anger and despair.
As I stand and watch him being prepared for his execution, the memory
of that day, when the hatred started, is vivid in my mind.
It began as any other, the baby waking first, hungry and demanding:
after his feed he lay smiling in his cot. and in between my daily chores,
the cleaning and fetching of water, I had the joy of watching my first
born son taking notice of the world around him.
But that joy was shattered by those marching feet, the cries of women,
the screams of children. Suddenly my house was full of noise; men
shouting, cruel steel with the marks of slaughter. My baby was
wrenched from me as I tried to protect him in my arms.
How can I forget that day? This man, was responsible for the death of
my baby; because of his birth my baby died. I have lived for this day,
when I could see him suffer, when I could be avenged for all my pain
and hurt. My life has been so full of hatred that there has been no room
for anything else, not family, not friends. Today I have come to glory in
his destruction. I cry crucify, crucify, crucify!
But, as I look up to his tortured face, his bleeding head and his nail
pierced hands, I am confronted by his forgiveness for my anger and
hatred. My heart is lifted by his compassion and love, out of the pit of
my self destruction. What have we done? We are destroying goodness
and love. I gaze up at that cross and see the face of Christ, my Saviour.'

*Marion E J Robinson*

## FAITH

'I see men like trees walking.'
The former blind man said.
'Life is sweet' thought Lazarus,
Brought back from the dead.
'This fish and bread's delicious'
Said the thousands who were fed.
The sick man obeyed the summons
'Rise up and take your bed.'
No wonder those who knew him
Followed where Jesus led,
For us in the twentieth century
We believe with heart not head
That all those centuries ago
For us, Christ's blood was shed.

*Margaret Bailey*


## TOUCH THEM LORD

They see no day, just constant night
Please Lord give, the blind their sight
Give the dumb speech, so they can talk
Touch the crippled Lord, so they can walk
Those with deafness, fill with cheer
Touch them Lord, so they may hear
Hungry people, Lord fill their need
Make their land fertile, for them to grow seed
Hear my prayer, Oh Lord above
Bless them all, with Your divine love
Bless us all, that we may be
Worthy of, the love from Thee
Touch us Lord, so we may rise
To dwell with You, in paradise.

*Peter Edward Waines Briggs*

# WHO WAS GUILTY?

''Twas I,' said the sparrow,
'With my bow and arrow . . .'

'I confess I killed the robin -
To my own eternal shame -
But if you'll only hear my story,
You will see I'm not to blame.

I've always been a poor chap
Working endless for my bread.
Then one day they shouted, *Sparrow!*
*We want the robin dead!*

At first I thought how can I?
For this robin is my friend!
But I knew whoever did it,
He'd still get it in the end.

And truly I can tell you,
It was hard for me to choose.
But they made me such an offer
That I didn't dare refuse.

So, you see, I am no murd'rer,'
Said the sparrow to the court.
'For it was not I that wished it,
But my services were bought.'

'So how much did they pay you?'
Asked the squirrel and the rat.
Then sparrow blushed and hung his head.

He didn't answer that.

*Elizabeth J Murray*

## MAN'S MIND

Man's mind is like a pit so deep
It has forgotten it had a beginning
Or ever will have an end.
Conscious only of the desire for
Self, which in its rise to power
Has thrust heedlessly down any motive
Opposing its path, which leads
It knows not where.
There is no aim for self,
No achievement, fulfilment or goal.
It ends where it starts.
Surely somewhere it achieves its aim?
The cry down the centuries pierces for a time
The gloom with expectancy.
Such wealth and power cannot just fade
Into oblivion, worthless.
In an obscure cavity of man's mind
The answer lies buried, smothered
By selfish desires, it whispers unheard,
There was a beginning - for
In the beginning God . . .

*Sylvia Michael*


## FLOWERS

Greeting the silver sun
Are rain-splashed flowers in bloom;
God's fairest sight but one,
A soul with grace-flowers strewn.

Scented with perfumes rare
Gently they sway to and fro
Fragrantly balming the air,
Kissing the winds that blow.

Cradled on clayey breast
Beneath eve's dew as it weeps,
Tired petals close and rest
Till the sun's eye opens and peeps.

So gay the part-hued bower!
So sweet the daisied sod!
So red the depth of a sword-shaped flower
Like the pierced Heart of God!

*Lily O'Reilly*


# LAST NIGHT I WALKED WITH JESUS

Last night I walked with Jesus
Over a pearl-lined bridge.
Softly trod out footsteps,
O'er mountain, hill and ridge.
We walked towards his tombstone.
To watch the people cry.
And as each head was risen
He blessed and passed them by.
We talked about the future
And spoke of yesterday.
I knelt down at his holy feet
For it was time to pray.
He led me to his birthplace
All bathed in ethereal light.
The shepherds followed closely
Behold, a wondrous sight.
We stepped out of the shadows,
To wave the moon goodbye
He bowed to kiss my forehead
Then vanished in the sky.

*Alison Davies*

## GOOD FRIDAY

Yes, I was there that day on Calvery.
I mingled with the throngs, I saw him fall.
I had no quarrel with the crowd's decree.

Why should I care some man was forced to haul
A heavy cross, while soldiers whipped and jeered?
He uttered not a sound, nor did he call

For help or water, though his face was smeared
With blood that trickled from a crown of thorns
Forced on by mocking men who spat and leered.

I felt no pity for him, merely scorn.
Watched clanging hammers nail him to the tree.
Yet, strangely, as he died I felt reborn.

I pondered this intriguing mystery;
Try as I would, I could not find the key.

*Kit Jackson*


## THIS IS MY TOMORROW

This is my tomorrow
Where dreams that once had died,
Consume me now in circles,
Whilst through my eyes I spy,
A pathway to our heavens,
Amidst clouds of virgin snow,
The lullaby of afternoon tide,
A better life to sow,
The gliding of the seagull,
Its piercing cry to hear,
A world of people laughing
And loving without fear.

*S Hexter*

## AITWE MUNGU

O, Lord, I long to hide myself in you,
Let me bury my head in your warm embrace,
For this world is full of hurt and pain - confusion seems to reign
And Lord, I need a hiding place in you.

Though crushed I take courage
Knowing you are crushed beside me,
Though bruised inside, I love you more
For you were bruised for me,
Though I'm aching and my heart is crying out to you
I rejoice for I know your ears are listening.

Hearts around me are so broken and so sore,
Souls close to me like open, bleeding wounds
And my own heart is so vulnerable and fragile
It's breaking for the load is hard to bear.

Though heartbroken I'm comforted
I know your heart is breaking too,
Though sore and bleeding I'm reassured
For you were wounded too,
Though weak and so vulnerable, I look to you for strength

Lead me on Lord, let me hold you by your hand,
Guide me through the rising waters and empty darkness
Hold me close and ensure I'm always watching you.
Keep me my Father, don't let me fall.

Though tempted I will stand
You know what I can bear,
Though always falling
You catch me - your arms are always there.
Though like a child in my weaknesses
I cling to you my Lord
Though alone, I surely know that's never true.

*Katherine Hogg*

## FLYING FAST

Time is of the essence,
so the saying goes.
It ticks, it tocks, it flashes by,
and where it's gone, who knows?

But do we make the most of it,
doing what is best?
Or is it 'oh so crowded'
that we cannot stop to rest!

The 'ifs and onlys' of our lives,
can leave us wondering why,
and suddenly we may just find
that life has passed us by!

Take time to stand and pause awhile,
consider what you do.
How wisely have you spent your time,
just how fulfilled are you?

The greatest gift that we can give
to each other, is our time,
and what a happier world this would be,
if that was done, sublime!

But we are busy everywhere,
rushing, racing fast,
trying to be first in line,
not letting others past.

'Be still and know that I am God,'
makes so much sense to me,
so take time out, reflect awhile,
and then I know you'll see.

*Jane Wade*

## THERE IS AN ANSWER

Dear one, I know the way you feel
The depths of pain, you can't reveal
The hollowness and helplessness,
The anguish and the deep distress,
How vulnerable your soul within
So sensitive to others' pain,
The trauma there from days long past
The grief and sorrow that still last.

But there's an answer to all this,
A healing that you must not miss,
A rest and joy there to be found,
A wholeness and a peace profound.

The Healer is the one who says:
'Come unto Me and learn My ways.
Kneel at My cross and let self die,
Yes, leave behind all that is *I* -
All that has happened hitherto -
The good, the bad, indifferent too.
Yield all to Me and let it go
Sin, sorrow, pain and all you know.
Empty yourself of everything
And let Me come to be your King.

For once My love has filled your heart
You'll find you've made a brand new start.
My grace and strength now dwell within
So I, in you, the battles win.
And from within I can impart
The love to heal your broken heart.
Receive then what it is I give -
*Abundant life* for you to live!'

***Mo Davies***

## PUNK

I saw a punk today
What a glorious sight
Standing in the ticket queue
In all her glory.
Purple and magenta hair
Standing up on end
Like a cock comb
Setting off her bright sharp face
With startling black eyebrows
Flashing eyes and sallow skin.
A dark pink coat set off the hair.
Tight drainpipe trousers
Purple high heels
Made up the picture.
She was proud, delighted
With the outfit and the
Impression she made.

Thank you, Lord
For exotic people
Who express themselves
In clothes and hairstyles.
We need peacocks and peahens
To give us a lift on drab days.
And also to give us courage to be bold and
Use these lovely colours and
Textures all given to us by you to enjoy.
Thank you Lord for exotic people.

*Jean Blight*

## FACE TO FACE WITH PERFECTION

Lingering over a carnation,
Carefully fashioned and sculpted,
Hand-painted origami,
White tinged with pink,
I sit enthralled by its breathtaking beauty,
Exquisite fragrance . . . and

. . . marvelling at Alpine peaks,
Majestically high and Creator-glorifying,
Unpretentiously proud,
Heads raised to Heaven,
I stand in awe of their towering immensity,
Silent strength . . . but

. . . gazing on you, my Lord,
I find immaculate purity . . .
Startling, blinding, heart-stopping,
Blazing holiness . . .
Devastating, terrifying, breath-catching,
Iridescent beauty . . .

. . . leaving me overawed, silent,
Freeing me from well-worn platitudes,
Transporting my soul into speechlessness.
Before you, Lord Jesus, words taper off . . .
Only adoration remains,
Face to face with *perfection*.

*K Chaplain*

## THE TREE

A beautiful tree small in stature
Yet somehow greater than all
Uniform in every way beautiful to behold
Bedecked in a fine array of leafage
I reached out touching the small branches
Its leaves soft and warm
From the rays of the bright sun
I felt drawn to it within it almost
As If I was in some way a part of it
Part of God's divine plan
To be there a guest at spring's awakening
God, never changes He renews constantly, ceaselessly,
With love always.
His nearness ever there, all around, in all things
Everywhere His divine love, fills the air
Close, closer than close.
Then could I give, this wonder, new to you,
That you could sense, and feel its inward glow,
Beautiful, like as the rose, when its petals unfolding thus
Bursts forth, its fragrances thrust,
And nostrils, drink it up absorbed,
Like as the radiance, of morning dew.

*Valerie Taberner*


## PERMANENT PEACE

Peace at last
It is declared
No more war
All happiness shared

We can agree
To live as one
Together beneath
A shining sun

Nothing could
We all agreed
Spoil our peace
It would succeed

There still is not
The slightest doubt
That peace between us
Will work out

*Peter Firth*


## THOUGHTS ON MILLENNIUM 2000 AD

Poets waxed lyrical almost hysterical
As on the skyline of London they gazed
The towers of Westminster, the Dome of St Paul's
The bells of St Clement's, the Tower with white walls
Magnificent buildings, bells always ringing
Carrying prayers, and praises up into the sky
Artists and artisans putting their souls in their buildings
Their thanks and their praises to 'The Father on high'
In 2000AD I wonder -
Will poets wax lyrical, almost hysterical
Over Lego-shaped skyscrapers and 'Millennium Dome'?
Machines without feelings do the shifting and lifting
Cold metals twisted oddly
Do not leave behind
A feeling of pride, and of prayer
And of praise for God's giving
Let's leave the mechanical
And get back to living.

*Nan Gosling*

## NO OTHER LOVE

So deeply loved were the ones that shone so bright,
in the mist of the morning light,
a love of splendour was within their dear hearts,
filled with a treasure of gentle charms.
Our hearts may ache, while our loved ones are far away,
no other love could ever take their place,
they are remembered every day, with so much style and grace,
they will hear us call out their names.
The words of love, *'I love you so!'* are very old,
they were written and told many years ago.
Farewell fills the stillness of the air, words are hard to find,
to be said, but with their love of faith, one day they will love again.
The years pass by, with the passing seasons some of those days contain
a very special meaning, maybe a memory of thought, is their sad reason.
The Holy Church stands upon a hill, there's always a warm welcome
that lies within, as voices are joining to sing, one of the early
morning hymns.
We thank our Lord, and God for this day, before we kneel,
and start to pray.
The flame of a candle shines so bright,
beside the Holy Book of eternal life.
The choir sings out the praises of the hymns,
in honour of our Lord Jesus' name.
Blessed are the words that are read and said,
as someone whispers in silent prayer,
to ask for loving tender care,
for someone who's in God's heavenly care.
May our love of faith always be honoured and adored,
until the day we return home O' Lord.
Bless the sadness of the mourners, for their love of emotion,
with their hearts filled with the love of devotion,
within the Church they will hear the written words,
about our Lord, the promised words,
*'Eternal life will always be yours!'*

The vision was the spirit of eternal life our saviour,
was our Lord Jesus Christ.
*There is a greater love of perfection, that awaits beyond,*
*in the limits of time, that place is yours, and mine!'*

**Fred Arthur**


## THE PLAN

Once there was designed a plan,
Ere the world could know its worth.
Or the sun and moon did span,
Day and night upon the earth.
Nor were earth's foundations formed,
Or waters on this planet's face.
No creatures, herbs or trees adorned,
Or from the dust the human race.

Infinite wisdom made this plan,
With love and mercy wrapped in grace.
In Godhead's scheme to rescue man,
And bridge the gulf of time and space.
Shall be achieved, the whole design,
Long purposed in eternity.
Death destroyed and God sublime,
True focus of fraternity!

And so agreed God's perfect word,
To be a lamb for sacrifice.
That when divine decree was heard,
To pay in whole transgression's price.
In full atonement, all complete,
This he did in flawless way,
To crush dark powers beneath his feet
And turn mankind's long night to day.

**P D Tollett**

## I BELIEVE

I hold the fragile flower and I see
Strong trade mark of divinity,
I walk barefoot on morning dew
And see nature fresh-created, new,
A rainbow's colours - I count seven,
Are there rainbows in His heaven?
Rainbows born from sun and rain,
Like mixing pleasure with some pain,
I see the shimmering insects fly,
Their dark shapes clear against the sky,
And walking slow on sandy beach
Crush shells pink-pearl or rosy-peach,
I hear the sea's deep-throated roar
Tossing waves to rocky shore,
I taste the fruit of the apple tree
And marvel this was made for me,
I smell wood smoke in autumn air,
Or rose scent rising like a prayer.

Oh, unbeliever, listen please,
And to your maker bend your knees,
Grand nature's parade is there to show
He is the way - the way to go,
Peace and love and beauty say
'He is the way, He is the way.'

*Ann Clowes*


## COUNT YOUR BLESSINGS

Count your blessings one by one,
God gave to our poor world His Son,
Gave freely that we might be free,
His Son who died on Calvery.

A gift so precious and so rare,
Why can we only stand and stare,
Why can't we give our lives to Him
When He knocks on your heart,
Just let Him in.

*Jean D Smith*


## THE FELLOWSHIP OF THE SPIRIT

Are you alone in darkness or in strife?
Has all the meaning drained away from life?
Do you face danger, illness or distress?
Is life's horizon simply wilderness?

In place of darkness let your life be filled
With light and comfort, and your torments stilled.
Talk with the Spirit, open wide the door,
Let God come in, have peace for evermore.

What a companion can the Spirit be,
Your own best friend for all eternity.
Hearts will be warmed and stirred to do God's will.
If you press on, His goals you will fulfil.

Invite the Spirit as a full-time guest,
Your life's potential will be manifest.
This very heartbeat showing you the way
To perfect fellowship that will not sway.

May this same Spirit permeate your life,
Rouse and enrich you, hopefulness be rife.
May all the world be fluent in the love
Of Jesu's Spirit sent as from above.

*Michael G Salmon*

## IN THE DARKEST PLACES

I walk down the street,
feeling so alone,
The world is all around,
It chills to the bone,
People cursed with blindness,
Use their poor false sight,
Carefully ignoring,
Their fiery plight.

Standing on the corner,
A man sells his goods,
Blissfully unaware,
This could lead to floods
Children so young,
Their innocence gone,
They feel no remorse,
For the things they have done.

People stand by thinking,
Can't make a difference,
But I know the truth,
I've found my deliverance,
The world around me,
It seeks something new,
I know the way,
It all lies with you.

I walk down the street,
No longer alone.

*Mark Milliken*

# THE STORY OF CHRIST

The Lord made the world
In seven days and said
Work for six days only
The seventh day you rest
And treat that day as holy

Six days you may have
To work and to be merry
But the seventh day
You will sing and pray
And keep that day as holy

Years later in the town of Bethlehem
A little babe was born
In a manger so they say
With animals all forlorn

He grew up and was worshipped
For the miracles he performed
Some people judged him wrongly
And to court he was called

The Judge he washed his hands of him
Do what you want he said
So they nailed him to a wooden cross
On a hill between two thieves

On the third day he rose again
So that all may know
Whoever turned to worship God
His love to them he'd show.

*J M Slowley*

## LOOK FORWARD UNTO ME

Look forward unto me
Thine trials are past,
Pain and suffer no more.
Fear not your future
Fear not your past,
Beginning and end are pure.
Mother and father and all akin
Friends and special love,
A few of the things I gave to you,
The symbol of peace, the dove.
The land of plants, of grass and trees,
Of animals and food to eat.
The sun and stars and falling rain
All beauty at your feet,
Let's not forget the power of prayer,
The moon and the power of the sea.
And when you close your eyes at last
Look forward unto me.

*William Lea*


## UNTITLED

My heart has been touched by Your hand, Lord,
Your forgiveness I know is there
- for me to take,
My life is guided by Your hand,
Your unconditional love I know is there
- for me to feel,
My unworthiness is lightened by Your hand,
Your healing powers - I know to trust
- But my faith wavers like corn in a breeze
Yet You are there - for *me*.

*Anne Harvey*

## GRIEVING

She awoke with a start in an unfamiliar place, the brilliant sun grinding into the back of her eyes. The ledge she lay on was narrow, clean rock with an opening into the mountain behind her, dark and unknown. Food and drink had been placed on the edge of the ledge, sufficient for her small need, and below the mountain fell sheer into a void. She blinked and reached forward to satisfy herself that she could still move. She ached. Sitting with the food, she contemplated the height and breadth and magnitude of the mountain.

As night fell, she turned her back on the drop below her, and pushed herself against the mountainside. The next morning she awoke cold and damp with dew, and resolved to look inside the cave for shelter. The darkness within the opening enveloped her more fully than the sunlight, and she stood for a while as her eyes became accustomed to the gloom. The cave did not reach back very far, and there was sand on the floor, enough to push into a comfortable pillow for her head. That night she slept in the cave.

The days passed. Every morning fresh food had been left for her, but she did not always have a hunger for it. She did not know where it came from or who delivered it in the dark night. But after a time, that ceased to trouble her. Days were spent watching the valley below and the mountain above. She became content with the pattern of her days; the sun rose each morning to bring warmth to the night dew, the food and drink were satisfying, her contemplation fulfilling.

She began to wonder if there were others above or below her, also sitting on ledges on the mountainside, considering their world's view. This thought brought her comfort. She might not be living her life alone or apart after all, but perhaps she was part of a dance, a circle of eternity, and some day she would rejoin others in that dance. But that was for the future.

*Dana Beney*

## THE GENTILES AND ISRAEL

We know from Scripture that the *Lord* has a special plan
concerning the Gentiles and Israel. He is the same *Lord* over both:
' . . . for there is no distinction between Jew and Greek.
The same *Lord* is *Lord* over all of us . . . ' (Rom 10v12)
So we have been called to share in a glorious future in the
Jerusalem above with Christ as the Head.
In the meantime, what is God's mind concerning Israel?
In Romans 11v11 we read that salvation has come to us Gentiles
*specifically to provoke Israel to jealousy*. This is written:
it is part of God's plan. It appears to me then, that this is why
God has chosen us Gentiles to benefit from the wonderful Gospel
of the Lord Jesus Christ: in His plan we have been called,
en masse, *precisely to provoke Israel to jealousy*.
Romans 11v8 tells us that it was God Himself who gave Israel
a 'spirit of stupor', so that most of them became callously indifferent
and blinded to the fact that Jesus is the promised Messiah.
Romans 11v25 tells that a temporary hardening has befallen
part of Israel until the times of the Gentiles are fulfilled,
and we are simply told in verse 26 that ' . . . and so all Israel
will be saved. As it is written: 'The Deliverer will come from Zion . . . '
There are movements afoot at the moment which seek to win Israel
to the Gospel. all I can say is 'May the *Lord's* will be done,'
but I also ask the question; is this fulfilling the Scripture
which states that the Gentiles will 'provoke Israel to jealousy'?
It seems to me that if someone is going to be provoked to jealousy,
they must see or hear about another having a relationship
with someone who is dear to them. Again this appears to be
backed up by Scripture. But I feel that this will truly happen
when Israel can see that our relationship with the Lord is so vital
and glorious and our love for each other so great
that their emotions will become incensed, as they realise that
*we have* what they unsuccessfully sought with their allegiance
to the Law.

At the moment the Jews are subject to two immensely profound aspects in the plan of God as defined in Romans 11v28:
'From the point of view of the Gospel, they (the Jews) at present, Are *enemies of God*, which is to your advantage and benefit.
*But from the point of view of God's choice* (election, Divine, selection) they are *still the beloved* (dear to Him) for the sake of their forefathers.'
So we see from this that there exists this tremendous *paradox:* on the one hand the Jews are still treasured by Him on account of His promises to Abraham, Isaac and Jacob.
So we Gentile Christians have our part to play in these things.
The Lord *will fulfil* what he has caused to be written, and we have to seek Him to reveal to us just how we fit in. Hebrews 6v1-3 tells us that we should proceed beyond the elementary stage in the teachings and doctrines of Christ. In other words, we must go beyond what we know of the saving grace of the Gospel, (whilst still maintaining strident evangelistic efforts) but go deeper as well into Spiritual matters and the 'solid food'. (Heb 5v12-14)

As it is written, the plan of the *Lord* is to provoke Israel to jealousy by means of the Gentiles.

*Franc Leyland*


## JESUS TO BE CRUCIFIED

If I must die do not despair
For I will always and forever be there
For you and all your earthly friends
No matter how much man alters the world's trends.
Just be true to our *Father* and to me
Then when I return you will all be set free
to live a heavenly life so great.
Just remember! I will be there if only you can wait.

*Jay Gee*

## An Easter Poem

You gave your life,
we gained our life,
our sins were many and now they are lost,
by your death you paid the cost.

Many thought you were dead and gone,
but you told people what would be,
You were doing a job that needed to be done,
saving a lost sinner like me.

Your Father sent you from heaven above,
to bring peace to men on earth,
You show people how to love,
People can now enjoy a new birth.

I'll always remember what you did for me,
upon the cross at Calvary,
you gave your all, that I might live,
show me always how to freely give.

*Jane Kenny*


## You

Your head is like a lighthouse,
Guiding the way.
Your eyes are as bright as stars,
Giving light each day.
Your mouth is like a river,
Full of precious words and truth.
Your heart is like a bar of gold,
With oozing love as proof.

*S Hoyle*

## THE OLD CHURCHYARD

The orchard lies next to the churchyard
On every bough and leaf
When raindrops fall from Heaven
It is as tears of grief.
The apple-scented blossom,
The new-mown grass so fresh
Remind me of long country walks,
The corn in fields to thresh.
The crooked branches lean over the wall
Into the churchyard's ground
And every spring life is reborn
Where peace a few have found.
The orchard is so pretty,
The perfume of her breath
Speaks of life and life reborn -
The churchyard leads to death.
The churchyard full of headstones,
The epilogue of life
Is beautiful - a gateway
From all tyranny of strife.
Her neighbour is our days on earth
When we should pick life's fruit -
The churchyard is where at the end
We lie asleep quite mute.
The churchyard has seen many a man
Come to Christ the King
Perhaps it's seen more life reborn
Than the orchard does each spring.

*Linda French*

## FAITH

Joy to the world we like to sing,
Heavenly praises to our King,
Joy in our hearts and praise in our hands
Our faith reaching out to other lands.
Praise in our prayer for Him on high,
Raising our eyes towards the sky.
Hoping that all who turn to Him
Will at last be relieved of all sin.
Turning to others we meet on the way
Saying 'Come on and join us and let us pray,'
Praise to God with grateful thanks and song
It's sure to help your life along.
Praise for all good things on this earth
Do your best and prove your worth.

*Joyce Hammond*


## UNTITLED

Be patient and your love will show
Be kind, and tender love will grow.
No envy means your love is true
No boasting and your love shines through.
Don't show pride or your love will wane
And when you're rude your love brings shame.
With love think not just of your own
May love dispel your anger shown.
Love forgets the wrongs of others
And shows not love to evil brothers
In truth does love rejoice so much
And protects you with a loving touch
So trusting in that certain love,
We have hope from our *Lord* above.

*A D Overton*

## IRREGULAR SYMPHONY
*(Reflections in St Mark's Venice)*

Secret corners of asymmetry,
Amiable juttings-out of gallery and pulpit,
Erratic slabs of marble agleam
In pink and grey, in roundel and rectangle;
Symphony of curves in every direction,
Arch and plant and pure motif,
Friendly space enclosed by geometry;
Melody of angles of light on gold mosaic,
Here a glow, there a shadow -
Glorious and insistent mixture.

Festive chorus of domes, pinnacles,
Statues, crosses,
Thrusting up into the intense blue sky,
Soaring above the generous embrace
Of arches and mosaics,
Of freshly-cleaned marble slabs and columns,
Revealing new colours in a rippling melody -
Your resonant praise surely touches the ear of God.

Such juttings-out and hidden corners,
Unexpected perspectives -
We find them also in our lives,
Odds and ends fitting together
Creating original compositions
With fascinating irregularities.
Age and situation bring their modifications -
Here an obsession, there a mannerism,
A conflict or the avoidance of one,
Then for a while things flow more smoothly.
God can take our jagged edges and our lack of symmetry:
Perhaps we are not irregular in His sight.

*Anne Sanderson*

## PRISONER

Manacled to the past,
With chains that outlast,
A human's frail years.
Fetters of steel will
Imprison me still,
In a cage of fears.

Night follows night,
No day intervening,
Evil succeeding.
Prayers never said
Go unanswered, so hope
Is extinguished.

Tramping the corridors of time,
My thoughts come into line,
Like sentries on duty.
My eyes shall see
The land afar off,
And the King in his beauty.

A dandelion clock
Floats on air,
As I watch it there,
A life seed broken away,
May it long stay
In my imagination.

*Sally Erskine*


## TO CARE

To care for other people
And maybe give them hope
Oh dear Lord hear my prayer
And give me strength to cope

To help all those around me
And never seek reward
To live my life for others
To show the world I care
Oh dear Lord help me
And listen to my prayer

*Gillian M Morrisey*


## JESUS OUR SAVIOUR

Jesus - our Lord, our Saviour,
You gave your life for us.
The day that you was crucified,
Nailed to a wooden cross,
Help us to get to know you,
Teach us to know you care,
That you are always here for us.
With others let us share,
The knowledge that you've given us,
To know every right from wrong,
In different situations, you help us to be strong,
Help us to never doubt you, and believe your every word,
Let these things be taught to others, and everyone be heard,
These blessings you bestowed upon us.
Is a special gift from you.
Let us help one another, the way you would like us to,
Let us take nothing for granted,
As we face each new day,
Let us just be thankful, you have shown us the way,
You are the way, the truth, the light,
And it will always beam.
So clearly it will show us to your pathway as you lead.
To follow in your footsteps, and to the way ahead.
Let us not forget that day, on that cross your blood was shed.

*Mary Cousins*

## THE UNSEEN PAINTER

You walk unseen
Throughout the world
Drawing back the curtain of the night.
The moon and stars.
Have lit the way.
To another day.

The dawn you paint.
With golden light.
The sun to shine,
To warm and make plants grow.
Dark clouds filled with rain.
To help them on their way.
Nourish seeds and plants.

To feed your world
And all its people
Unseen you walk with each and everyone.
Your hand upon their shoulder.
Leading the right way to go
It's not easy, you too well know.

With arms outstretched.
You embrace mankind.
How hard it must be
To try to quell the unrest and hopelessness,
Of all your people.

They cannot see.
How hard you've worked.
To make the world,
As you would like it to be,
Flowers, trees, birds, fish,
The mountains, rivers and seas,
For all to share
All people to be free.
From want,
From fear,
From hunger
A home for everyone.

Oh! Help us Lord,
To be what you,
Would have us be.

*Joy Peart*

## LOVE

What God has joined together
Let no man pull apart
No matter how they try to
They'll never break our hearts

My love for you will see me through
These long and lonely days
And God above with all His love
Will always find a way

I hope my love for you
Will keep you strong
Time will pass and it won't be long
Before I hold you in my arms and say
I love you with all my heart.

*S Croft*

## THE EMPTY CROSS

Could we have borne the sight of Jesus on the cross,
Hanging there in agony,
To see the cruel thorns,
His nail-pieced hands and feet?
How blessed are we to witness the empty cross.

Could we have withstood the Power of God,
The terror, when the sky turned black,
When the earth shook, the rocks split
And the temple curtain tore in two?
And say, 'Surely, He was the Son of God.'

Could we have overcome the grief of the women
At the sight of His open tomb?
'They have taken away my Lord.'
What dread to see the shining angel,
What joy to share the good news, 'Jesus is risen.'

Will we share the disciples' fear and rejoicing
When Jesus comes to us again?
Or will we doubt the existence
Of the Saviour, as Thomas did?
Will we shout 'Crucify,' as the world is crying.

Christ must be buried deep under the weight of our sins,
As He was for those three dark days,
Our Lord needs to be raised again
From the tomb of this world, today.
Can our love roll that stone away to welcome our King?

Looking at the empty cross our hearts must fill with love
Overflowing as tears long gone,
When Christ was 'high and lifted up',
Let us rejoice and worship God
Who forgives our sins through His only Son's precious blood.

*H N Smitheman*

## PROGRESS

Fear not science, nor deny
what could enlighten searching eyes.
Often, God will web His wonders,
through the wisdom of the wise.

Just be certain, of these sages,
use a reasonable head,
for the truths, that stand secure,
will never ever prove Him dead.

Facts, locked fast, back in the past
may rate 'tomorrow's world', unreal.
But, it simply adds enhancement
to God's greatness, with His seal.

Vast, galactic bangs, or crunches,
stars disintegrating, run
whirlpool peaks to quantum leaps.
Tomorrow's old, beneath the sun.

So, don't be alarmed, my friend,
if science forces a review,
what is false will ultimately
always prove itself untrue.

*Nothing robs God of His glory.*
*So, lift up those troubled eyes,*
*And remember who it is*
*Apportions wisdom, to the wise.*

**Pearl**

## THE PATH OF LIGHT

As I walk towards the path of light
With love and strength so pure, so white
The spirit of angels guiding me through
Like my own special journey, my own special pew
The congregation's love that I do bring
The music so sweet, the prayers we sing
For the love of Jesus the Son of God
Thanking for the temple and the fisherman's rod
The knowledge of faith, hope, charity and love
Freedom of speech, the wings of a dove
I hear the spirits' voices so sweet
Welcoming me the handshakes when we meet
Wealth, riches and honour I do not need
As my heart feels beauty, love, plenty to feed
I share my feelings, my love, my strength
To all on the path one in tenth
Towards the light my wings take me
Like a magnet with honey attracting the bee
There in the bright yellow light
Stands my Father, my God, my true delight
Just like life the path is straight
If you obey the rules don't make a debate
Don't look for doubts or they'll be found
Keep the faith, spread the word around.

*Sandra Cushnaghan*

## FATHER?

Did Isaac ever trust his Father Abraham again?
After that outing
to the mountain,
Hand in hand up Mount Moriah.
Carrying firewood
Helping Father,
Puzzled questions
'Where's the lamb?'

Trust again when Father Abraham
Bound him
Laid on top of pyre,
Reached for knife
And nearly killed him.
Only voice of angel calling
Stopped the slaughter.
'Here's the lamb.'

Shaky walk
Down Mount Moriah
Back to open arms of Sarah.
Lamb in place of son
Lay burning.
But did Isaac trust
His Father Abraham
Again?

*Sue Smith*

## REMEMBER

Remember the mocking which He endured
  Rejection pain and scorn
    Upon the cross at Calvary
     Hung Jesus all forlorn

Remember the nails that pierced His hands
  That held Him to the tree
    Battered and bruised His body hung
     On the cross for you and me

Remember the thorns that crowned His head
  That we may be set free
    What held Him to the cross that day
     Was His love for you and me

Remember the whips that tore His flesh
  And the sword that pierced His side
    It was His love for sinful man
     That's why the Saviour died.

*Frank Mulrooney*


## LET THE WORLD COME TO CANA

Let the world come to Cana,
For a great Millennium feast,
With food and wine in plenty
For greatest and for least.

Let the world come to Cana,
Eat, drink, be merry,
In memory of Jesus
And His matchless mother Mary.

Let the world come to Cana,
Where water was made wine;
Of Christ's astounding master plan
A foretaste and a sign.

Let the world come to Cana,
Christian, Muslim, Jew;
To conquer ancient enmities,
'Whate'er He tells you, do.'

*Michael Gaffney*


## UNTITLED

Set your hearts and minds
on things above
Where Christ is seated
at the right hand of God.
Put to death the old
and live in the new
And God will pour His
blessings on you.
Clothe yourselves with compassion
humility and love
Bear with one another,
learn to forgive.
Let the peace of Christ
be in you,
Live in His word
rejoice with thanksgiving
Giving glory to God.

*Margaret Dolman*

## AND THE LAME SHALL DANCE?

Will You make me better, Lord,
Will You do it today?
It's all that I'm asking for
Now that I've come to pray.

Will You make my toes straight, Lord?
Will You take the scars away?
Can I have a foot-shaped foot?
Lord, what do You say?

I know You can make me better;
You made the lame to dance.
Please do it one more time, Lord,
Let me have a chance.

You can put a stop to these infections;
You can make me as good as new
And then I can do what I've never done
I could wear a normal shoe

And then I could dance to my heart's content
And run the London marathon
And climb Mount Everest
And it would be, oh so much fun!

And who knows what else I could do?
I could do almost anything;
I would skip round the world six times Lord
And boy, would they hear me sing!

But is it all a dream, Lord?
Is healing in Your plans for me?
If Your answer's 'No,' Lord
Let me accept what You want me to be

Because that's the hardest part, Lord
It's not something I can easily do;
I don't like being beaten
But I *could* make an exception for You!

*D G Bulsara*


## WHAT DO YOU THINK OF CHILDREN?

What do you think of children?
As a Christian do you care?
Do you know the hurt and anger
That they sometimes have to bear.
Are you aware of the secret tears they shed
For the dysfunctional life their parents have led?
Do you see their bad behaviour?
Do they shout and scream and swear?
Have you taken time to tell them,
About the unconditional love, Jesus has to share?
Have you explained about that new beginning
No matter what they've done?
For God took away all their sins,
The day man crucified his Son.
So as you walk your Christian path
And see a child in need,
Just take the time to listen
To that young person's needs.
Try not to sympathise on Sunday
And forget their needs by Monday,
But clothe them in the love of God
And guide them in His ways,
For the precious blood of Jesus
Has washed their sins away.

*Kate Brearley*

## REFLECTIONS FROM FENLAND

The wide spaces of Fenland welcome the incomer as God's heavens will welcome the believer.
I see the splendour of God's creation in the big skies, the shimmering water of the rivers and drains; the fertile soil bringing forth crops of sugar beet, of carrots and parsnips too big for the delicate tastes of southern counties' supermarkets, of strawberries so delicious that their taste alone is evocative of manna from heaven. In spring, field on field are filled with glorious yellows and creams of daffodil and narcissus followed by the multicoloured beauty of tulips and then roses.

But then this Eastertide came heavy rains filling the rivers until they spread over their banks, drowning the washes and submerging village, town and farm. Providing another opportunity for people to say 'Why Lord? Why us?' There are those who would point to the floods and say they are indicative of a vengeful god inflicting punishment for the ills of the nation; but why punish by the destruction of beauty, why not take vengeance to the sordid areas of inner cities where those who practise crime are found and the god of materialism
is rife?

I ponder, is there another answer to 'Why?' If we are created in God's image then can God also be imperfect though striving for perfection? Should we not remember that it is not just this small planet earth that he holds in his care but the myriad planets and stars of the universe and does he find the task of controlling the distribution of rainfall on planet earth so that there are no floods in Fenland nor famine in Africa as difficult a task as I find it difficult to thread a fine needle with cotton and sew straight stitches?

Can we not take comfort from a God who knows our weaknesses and imperfections so well, that judgement is tempered with forgiveness. Thus we are enabled to give thanks for floods that bring with them the chance of renewal, the forging of community spirit and the opportunity to re-evaluate what is really important in our lives.

*Pamela Mundy*

## ALL SORTS

People from West Belfast
Are as cold as glass
  So they say
    But hey
      I've known a few
        Who could tell a story or two
        And could be used
          If they so choosed
          By the Master.

The boys from Glasgow town
Have scars 'A' crown
  I've been
    So therefore I've seen
      Plenty of hard men
        Have been born again
        And believe it or not
          Have given all that they've got
          For the Master.

Ballymena's the Bible belt
But God's better 'felt' than 'telt'
  So we go
    And try to show
      That you and me
        Can be free
        As hand-in-glove
          Is peace and love
          From the Master.

*Davie Erwin*

## THE GIFT

A precious gift of life
Placed in my hands.
I held him for the first time.
Pure Joy.
Perfect.
Perfect hands, perfect feet.
His creased, bloodied face
Crowned with natural glory.
No modesty, though naked.
The only blush, that of life.
His beating heart, his warmth,
Mine.

In my hands I hold the life,
Of another,
A new life, fresh life,
Untouched.

*Elizabeth Everton*


## I REFUSE TO GO

I will never leave you all,
therefore I refuse to die.
I will be that sparkle,
in the cold night sky.
I will be the shining sun,
and spread my generous light.
I'll also be watching -
through your souls at night.
I will be that winter robin -
who ventures amongst the snow.
So whenever you remember me,
remember that I refuse to go.

*Vicki Watson*

## WHOM SHALL WE SEND?

'Whom then shall we send
And who will for us go
Out into the vineyard,
The seeds of life to sow?'

This plaintive cry that echoes,
Calling from the past,
Will always want an answer,
So long as life shall last.

It is calling to me,
But I'd rather not know,
And sending me out
Where I'd rather not go.

If someone went in my stead
I'm sure they'd do just fine,
But should I ask others to carry
The burden that is mine?

Still the voice is speaking,
Persuasive, in my ear.
'Won't you do it, just for me,
I'm at your side, what should you fear?'

So I take up my burden gladly,
Thinking of those now above,
Who strove years ago to show me
The grandeur of His love.

'Whom then shall we send?'
May this our answer be,
Each time we hear Him calling,
'Lord, here am I, send me.'

***Revd F Hutchinson***

## LOVE - TALKING TO GOD

I found it first Lord
In what my friends had to say.
In my mother and father
Around every day.

In a walk in the woods
With my brothers
And me swinging up high in a great oak tree.

In the birth of my child
Who, then sat on my knee
Strong and sure and guided by me.

In the rhythm of life,
The sun, the air, the sea
In a tree budding forth
Shaking winter to the ground.

I saw it in a disabled child's smile
His fingers' shaky grip
His dependence all the time.

I found it in a conversation
When blackness was all around
When I was small and lost
Trodden into the ground.

Then a hand reached out
And I knew you were there.
I found love Lord today.

Spreading out
Like the branches of the great strong tree
You taught me Lord
Love is first to be found in me.

**Bernadette Neave**

## HOPE

When problems get too great for us,
We feel we cannot cope,
We turn to our Redeemer,
Our one and only hope.

False prophets will deceive us
Such as the horoscope,
But He will never let us down,
Our one and only hope.

The scientist may isolate
The latest isotope.
For good or ill? Who is to say?
Our one and only hope.

The lottery, the cigarette,
The alcohol, the dope
Will not bring lasting happiness;
For that in vain some hope.

The Bishop and the Parish Priest,
The Minister, the Pope
Are worthy men but sinners all
But Christ is their true hope.

While men reject the Gospel truth,
In darkness they will grope.
We pray that they will see the light
And grasp their one true hope.

**Graham Winterbourne**

## GOD RULES

God rules over the morning,
In the east He commands the sun to rise,
He gives hope with each new dawning,
For all His ways are wise.

God rules over the flowers,
Tells them from each seed the way to grow,
He gives peace beneath each bower,
On men His blessings He does bestow.

God rules over all creation,
Taught the animals their playful ways,
God rules over every nation,
He has numbered all their days.

God rules over the sky at night,
The moon and stars they shine at His behest,
He keeps us safe within His sight,
As we lay down to take our rest.

Why not let God rule in your heart,
Listen - hear Him knocking at the door,
To us His love He does impart,
With Him we'll dwell for evermore.

*Pauline Wilkins*


## YOUR LOVE

Your love poured down from Calvary's Hill,
It's pouring now and always will.
Reaching for the sad and lost
Redeeming blood of priceless cost.
You died to take our sins away
To open up heaven's highway.

*Cathy Stokes*

## COMMUNION

'O Father, let not this cup pass from me,'
We pray, not as your Son prayed in his grief,
Embodying the pain of honesty.

We drink his blood, we say uncertainly;
Lord, I believe - help thou my unbelief.
O Father, let not this cup pass from me.

We taste the chalice; he gulped agony.
The heavy sweetness on our tongue is brief,
Embodying the pain of honesty.

Lord, lead us further in the mystery,
Deep down, far out, to sorrow's furthest reef -
O Father, let not this cup pass from me! -

Where, wrecked, abandoned, we at last may see
And touch and love you with that common thief,
Embodying the pain of honesty.

The wisdom bleeding from the bitter tree,
The life that drips from every sword-edged leaf -
O Father, let not this cup pass from me,
Embodying the pain of honesty.

*F J Dunstan*


## METAPHYSIC

I have this sense
Perhaps I mean feel
Our common language
Is no longer adequate
To express what I feel
Perhaps I mean sense
About, me, you, them, it.

*N W Parker*

# A SIMPLE

A simple woman, Mary,
gave birth to a God-man.
A simple-looking baby
made the universe with his bare hands.
A simple adolescence
that any other child could relate to.
A simple-looking man
with a power way beyond any me or you.
A simple loaf of bread
He increased for the supplying of a whole gathering to feed.
A simple bowl of water
He took to turn into wine for a whole reception's plead.
A simple cane of wood
He took and used for His dying,
to bring us the salvation and only form of life that we need.
A not so simple death
which made the whole world shake and start thundering.
A not so simple act
which made the Roman guards start wondering.
So simple the creation,
two thousand onward years from then, now in our time.
Still simple are the minds
which state far too intellectual, so leave behind.
Today we're left with a simple set belief which has resulted
in Christianity, for us to live and love it.
Yet man sees through it as only standing fairytale,
and has to go above it.
So simple is the second coming then,
when we've no feet to stand.
So simple, you the heathen now,
and when taken from this land.

*Debra C Kuppers*

## THE GIFT OF SIGHT

What a blessing the gift of sight,
To see the words I read and write.
Look at the faces of those I love.
Gaze at the stars and moon above.
Admire the beauty of plant and flower,
Refreshed in colour by April shower.

What a blessing the gift of sight,
To watch the sun pour forth its light.
To see the fruits on leafy trees,
And yellow corn brushed by a breeze.
Falling flakes laying carpet of snow.
Recognise the places where'er I go.

What a blessing the gift of sight,
To see a baby smile with delight.
Able to choose the clothes I wear.
Look into a mirror to brush my hair.
To walk about with carefree stride,
Without assistance of a guide,

What a blessing the gift of sight,
And if I close my eyelids tight,
Just as the blind I cannot see
The obstacles in front of me.
So when my spirits need a lift,
I think of those without the gift,
And with those thoughts I realise,
How blessed I am with seeing eyes.

*Harry M M Walker*

# THE STORM

The rain it came
In thunderous roar,
It swept away my village
Until it was no more
Its angry bellows sounded
Loud and fierce
In screaming rage and fury
Ever near
The fear within me rose
I trembled violently
I'd never known such fear
Could ever be
I prayed. 'Dear Lord, Dear Lord
Please take good care of me'
At last, abatement sounded
All around
I fell on my knees, with head bowed
To the ground
In grateful thanks
That I'd been spared
And knew my prayers
Had all been heard

*C O'Donnell*

# LIFE

I sit and think and wonder why
For all those years life passed me by
I stood aside and watched it pass
Years went by, it passed so fast
So many thoughts, so many tears
Such loneliness for all those years

That void that dwelled within my heart
Empty was that missing part
I tried to fill the emptiness
With many things that led to stress
But that instant thrill just didn't last
The fun and frolics faded fast
Each time I stopped and took a breath
I was reminded of the stench of death
I tried to run and tried to hide
But you can't escape what attacks inside.

So I found you Lord and what was odd,
The answer all along was God.
I'm joyous now that I've been saved,
And my road to heaven paved.
Thank you Lord for answered prayer.
Thank you Lord for being there.
I even thank you Lord for strife,
And for all the troubles in my life,
For all the days when things go wrong,
For heavy burdens made me strong.
Now by my side, you'll always be,
Thank you Lord for saving me.

*Victoria McLeod*

## MOTHERHOOD

Being a mother is wonderful.
Being a mother is great
What else can I say as I look
All around me and think 'What a state'!
There's more grass in the kitchen than outside
The living room's scattered with toys
But where would I be without them
My baby girl and two lovely boys?

Steven's first, he's six and at school now
Learning quickly to read and to write
Nathan's next, three, and full of mischief
He stands on his dinosaur to turn on the light
Rebecca's the baby, and beautiful
Eight months now and learning to crawl
Growing up with two big brothers
She already seems wise to it all!

I look in the mirror and sometimes
Can't believe I'm the mother of three,
But I say thanks to God every day
That he showered these blessings on me.

*Carole Walker*


## LAKELAND

Evening mists encircle trees,
Round the lake white swans asleep,
In the twilight quickening breeze
Cools the gorse on hillsides, steep.

High above the blue lake, looming,
Old, grey granite rocks abound,
Living rockeries, richly blooming,
This the Heaven I have found.

Stone walls section grazing meadows,
Tiny hamlets hide away,
Towering peaks cast lengthy shadows,
Snow-capped on a winter's day.

Home of hawk, majestic eagle,
Fox and badger, timid deer,
In this land of mountains, regal,
I am sure that God is near.

*Eric Holt*


## UNTITLED

The poppy fields of Flanders
Are stirring once again
With glowing rich, red beauty
Like war's scarlet battle stain
Voices echo far away in some distant
Vale of time peaceful now the tired ones
Who faded in their prime
Whose faces blur in time's embrace
Like seasons long ago, that seemed forever
Sun-blessed with memory's sympathetic glow

The harvest field in rich, red cloak
Is a reminder to us all
How mighty were those selfless ones
Who honoured us with bravery
Before their final call
Now winds convey their silence
Their courage speaks again, in Flanders'
Lonely poppy fields, they bloomed but not in vain.

*Albert Edward Reed*

# PEOPLE

There are people who have plenty there are people who have none
And people who have just enough to help to carry on
There are people who are pretty and people who are plain
And those who are just in between whether Jack or Jane
There are people who are grumpy and people who are kind
But both have got a bit of both in this old world I find
There are those of us with courage when illness comes along
And those who simply cannot cope whatever may be wrong
There are tall men there are short men there are fat men there are thin
There are those who always have a scowl and those with silly grin
Some people are born stupid some people are born bright
There are people who are greedy and want everything in sight
There are people who are noisy and people who are quiet
There are those who always eat too much and others on a diet
There are people who are generous giving everything they've got
And those who are as mean as hell and keep the flaming lot
Some folk are keen as mustard to reach the very sky
And others who are quite content to let life pass them by
There are bigots and eccentrics there are thieves and liars too
There is cruelty and cunning and those who misconstrue
The world is full of hatred full of deeds that make you sad
And then you find a mass of good that far outweighs the bad
For even though the world is full of every kind of deed
One still can find the sweetest soul to help when one's in need
For each of us I know is true is made by God above
And all are individuals and everyone needs love.

*Barbara Hampson*

## SILENT LOVE

If words should ever fail thee
in times of great distress,
And silence is the hammer -
your strength put to the test,
remember that in silence
resides the word of God,
and silence is the Truth,
that trusty measuring rod,
in which one places perfect faith,
a shining love unmasked,
beyond all words, all thoughts and deeds
a heart that never asked.
Silence, then, is Holy,
so in its arms rejoice,
and to love's great bearing
never once let loose thy voice.

*Ian Lee Armer*


## A HINT OF FORGIVENESS

Bright light, halo, God's life-saving tree,
In the net of the Angel, she catches me,
Did I stray just for a while?
Innocence I see in her peaceful smile,
Glimpsing lost memories for me she has found,
Just for a while I let myself down,
In my guilt, I ask, if I can be set free,
From the burdens of shame I carry with me,
Feather light is her touch,
That soothes my worried brow,
Surely this may be for me a sign,
That the Lord may forgive me now.

*Elaine Hawkins*

## PEACE

Peace is a beautiful word
With sincere loving and gentle care,
If only it could stretch
To all nations everywhere!

Even among families
No grumbles, rows or complaint,
More caring and aid for each other:
Though no-one of course, is a saint.

Think of the symbols of peace;
The delicacy of the peace rose;
The beautiful, graceful dove;
Fine symbols are both of those.

So try to emulate these
And a more peaceful world should survive,
Then people perhaps would feel
It's a joy to be alive!

*Marjorie Cowan*


## EMOTIONS

What an emotional year, this one has been,
With so many happenings, much emotion I've seen,
We all have emotions and laugh till we cry,
but whatever does happen, time just passes by.

Emotions are given to each one and all,
The good and the bad, the short and the tall.
Without our emotions what would life really be,
With no shouts of joy or smiles to see.

And if I didn't listen, to what my heart says,
I'd be in trouble in so many ways,
For it keeps me aware that god is still there,
And whatever does happen, I know that he'll care.

For dead is the person when emotion's not there,
But alive are the ones who show that they care,
For it makes us remember that god's over us all,
And the tears that we cry, are good for the soul.

*M A Atkinson*


## LIFE'S JIGSAW PUZZLE

Even though all our lives are all interwoven in this huge scenic game
We are still just tiny parts of the pieces for the puzzle to frame
So to find one's place in the pattern man tries so hard to unfold
The plan of a secret - the deepest mystery to hold.
Forever searching and seeking for our knowledge to grow
To learn that the start and the ending comes from believing - to know
That sometimes God in His wisdom also joins in the play
To help or to hinder, until finally our picture to lay.
Although our life now may be over, never again to be seen
Unless we can enter somewhere else in the scheme,
But to appear in this new picture we must have loved and shown care
For those who are lost in the shadows - their misfortunes to share,
So with eyes born to see, find in your spirit to give
All the love and affection for as long as you live
For if love's spectrum of bright colours is the life that we make
Then the soul that lies sleeping will at the ending awake
To a life everlasting where all darkness shall fade
If the picture is love from the life we have made.

*Eric Day*

## TRAPPED

Little bird, oh little bird, how did you get here?
You see there are no open doors, nor windows open near.

And yet you find yourself so lost, how fearful you must be,
oh little bird be still a while and let me set you free.

Won't you still your tiny wings, and let them rest for now?
And calm your beating heart inside, if your fears allow.

for look an open skylight, I opened it for you,
so let me be your guiding hand, to see you safely through.

I promise I shan't hurt you, my hands will be so kind,
for they knew pain so piercing once, but I had you in mind.

And gently gently up you go, now fly on freedom's wing,
and as you go you're not alone, as our hearts join and sing.

*Kathy Earlam*


## MY HEAVENLY FATHER

I've got faith in my Heavenly Father
I trust Him in everything
He's given His promise so I would rather
Follow Him than my own selfish sin.
I've got hope in my Heavenly Father,
His son died for all our sins
To show His love so we gather
To praise Him in everything.
There's beauty all around us
Given by God's own hand.
Let's thank Him with alleluias
And follow His faithful band.

*Mary Bird*

## THE SERVICE

The summer months are almost gone, the time for me to go draws near,
And no more shall we look upon the friend who recently trod here.

St Bridget's kirk is grey and old,
And four square on its gentle hill,
Whence Cumbrian lands stretch fold by fold,
With sheep-grazed slopes and vales to till.

We pause beside the outer gate,
Whose name denotes mortality;
A minute there the bearers wait . . .
Then upward walk, and so do we.

We hear old words from holy writ
Preceding ere we go within,
Observing customs long found fit
By friends who kneel with kith and kin.

We pray, think private thoughts, and sing,
And every pastoral sentence heed
For every comfort it may bring
To kinsfolk in the greatest need.

We warm towards the words that grope,
And know them as the most sincere,
But listen for the phrase of hope,
Assuaging loss of what was dear.

We see again the Cumbrian skies, we see mortality interred,
And old folk-ways that symbolise the faith that dwells in
deed and word,
We lift our eyes unto the hills, where truth and beauty
still reside;
We see the peaks as sunlight spills to aching hearts that
yet abide.

*Philip J Burchett*

## THE HEAVENLY CROWN

It's not what we possess
But what we are that counts;
It's not in material things
We gain the heavenly crown.

It is in quiet simple ways -
A walk along a country road,
The inspired song of a bird
The caress of the first white rose.

In humble lowly pursuits
We find our souls take flight -
A glimpse of a flowing brook,
The star studded sky at night.

It may be in a village church
As on bended knee we pray,
Or the clasp of a baby's hand
We reach the heavenly way.

If we truly seek Him
God bestows His gifts renown
The price was paid on Calvary -
'Tis the glorious Heavenly crown.

*Elsie M Childs*

## LIFE IN CHRIST

The path of Christ will always be,
Paved with gold, for you and me.
Days of beauty shining through,
Nothing to mar, or spoil our view.

Daily, as we rise and shine,
We cherish every moment thine.
Our love for you, will never end,
As you are our loving friend.

You treat us special everyday,
When we heed to what you say,
How we love you, Jesus dear,
As we feel your presence near.

Our life, our hope, our everything,
For us, you carry on your wing.
Into your tender arms we stay,
Protected, sheltered, from harm's way.

*Barbara Elsie Bernadette Uttley*

## GOD'S GIFT OF LIFE

So much we take for granted
In the busy lives we lead,
Yet we should spare a moment
To dwell on all the Lord decreed.

We should be kind to others,
Help them all we can,
Tend the sick and unfortunate,
Let us love our fellow man.

Give thanks for nature's beauty,
For the food upon our table,
Rejoice in God's gift of a new-born babe,
Pray this new life will grow strong and able.

Let us be forgiving,
Guide the sinners on their way
To a better Christian way of life
Before the judgement day.

If we follow our Lord's teaching
Then we will not be sad
Because joy and love will fill our lives,
For the life God gave, give thanks, be glad.

*Barbara Sowden*

## TAKE MY HAND

Take my hand, dear Lord, as I rise this day
Lead me forward to face anew
The daily tasks, as I make my way
With Thine hand in mine, Thy way so true.

Take my hand, dear Lord, let me not ask
Why a new burden, I must bear
The load may be heavy, an unusual task
Maybe a sorrow with many a tear.

Take my hand, dear Lord, give me Thine aid
Knock at the door, please enter in
Lift me up, that all the sorrows fade
Give me strength, that I may be free from sin.
Take my hand, dear Lord, though the road be long
As Thy will be done, make my life
Of Thy many blessings, may there be song
At the end of the road, no more strife.

Take my hand, dear Lord, lest I should fall
Or stumble on the way,
Open mine ears, to hear Thy call
To listen what Thou would'st say.

With Thine hand in mine, I'll see the way
The Truth, the Light, Thy Glory,
Ask it will be given, Thou did'st say
When on this Earth, was told the story.

*Sylvia G Poore*

## A ROSE AMONGST THORNS

The Head's awake,
The trumpet is yet to sing;
Pierced petals of divinity
To an executioner secured.
Words of wisdom and love spoken
Even though his life ebbing away,
Lost in moments of solitude,
Parental eyes cast aside.

The Head falls,
The trumpet's about to sing;
A moment of silence surrounds,
Awaking the watching crowd.
They see a broken stem
Supported by its executioner
Who stands fast, rugged,
Celebrating another victim.

The Head hangs,
Winter's final note;
A moment of realisation touches
Those who view a crown of thorns.
With the withering of the leaves
Death takes his grip,
*Its blossom falls and*
*Its beauty is destroyed.*

**Gerald Thomas Wall**

## OUR LORD OUR FATHER

Our Lord, Our Father,
This day we turn to You,
To help us with our pain.
So here ever-after,
With hearts so pure and true,
We endeavour to face another day.

Through Your son you taught us,
That on You we can depend,
So long as we keep within Your faith
And constantly to remind us,
Your spirit You do send,
To help us to keep to Your way.

So Father though we suffer,
At this time of our loss,
We know You'll always help us through,
In our life there is no other,
Who can help to count the cost,
That's why this day we turn to You.

So now Father in conclusion,
It just remains to say,
Just how deeply we rely upon Your word,
Though each day we find confusion,
As we try to find our way,
But through You we're always reassured.

*Paul Secrett*

## UNTITLED

Blessed Jesus - Light divine
Enter in this soul of mine
Let your spirit from within
Keep me pure and free from sin

Blessed Jesus - Holy Dove
Sepulchre of truth and love
May my doubting spirit know
Love from springs - which overflow

Blessed Jesus - Saviour dear
Ever constant - always near
Beacon for the stormy tossed
My northern star when I am lost

Blessed Jesus - Prince of peace
Troubles never seem to cease
Those healing powers You freely give
Come down - O Lord - with man to live

Blessed King of all creations
We need You Lord - unite the nations
That we on earth can clearly see
The fruits of being One-in-Three

Abba-Father - love paternal
Jesus - brother - love fraternal
Holy Spirit of priceless worth
New life - new peace - new love - new birth.

*E Dobson*

## LAY YOUR BURDENS DOWN

'Come lay your burdens here,'
He softly says to me,
'That they will no longer drag you down
But free your life from all anxiety.

I have paid the price
You no longer need to struggle,
Oh, if you would just lay them down,
You would know My peace and serenity.

Do not pull them back
Once laid at My feet, entrust them fully to me.
I will take care of them
And in so doing, I will take care of you.

Come, to the foot of the Cross,
Where you can leave all things with Me.
I will work them out
For I have your best interests at heart.

Then, once you've laid your burdens down
You will be able to walk on, in freedom
And you'll learn anew the peace which comes
From leaving all things unto Me.'

*Melanie Booth*


## WERE YOU THERE?

Were you there - did you see the brilliant light
that shone to point the way for them?
Were choirs of angels praising Him on sight
when men reached that lowly place in Bethlehem?

Then say - in silent homage on that special night
did you see oxen bending - on the nod?
Came three kings with gifts - so wise - so right
to celebrate the birth - this Child of God?

Say, were you there to see it all unfurled,
the rare glory of this joyous peaceful scene?
Miracle of this babe sent to love the world
that knew him not - nor cared a bean.

Then spread the good news for all to share,
that sleeping infant lying in the holy manger
was born to save mankind. Praise him in prayer,
give thanks if you were there, dear stranger.

*Lena Cooper*

## THE SPARROW'S FLIGHT

A mission came to the English,
To offer hope beyond the grave,
Telling the words of Jesus,
And how he had come to save.

Paulinus told an English king,
And an old counsellor spoke up:
'Life is but a sparrow's flight
In the bright hall where we sup,

With fire alight on the hearthstone,
And outside the falling rain.
The bird flies in at one door,
Pauses, then flies out again.

A moment in the light and heat,
Then out in the winter's cold!
What comes before or after
We know not, nor have been told.

If this new teaching can tell us,
Then let us gladly follow,
Rejoicing in the precious gift
That frees us all from sorrow.'

*Valerie Venables*

# CONSIDER THE DIFFERENCE

Consider the difference between cradle and cross
and gaining and losing and profit and loss
a baby to visit and gifts brought with love
and a man, hurt and bleeding, eyes lifted above.

Consider the difference between welcome and hate
being showered with gifts and then left to your fate
washing friends' feet, breaking bread, drinking wine
Then disowned and deserted 'He's no friend of mine'

Consider the difference between Jesus and men
the one living for others, the others living for when
the mortgage is paid, and our boat has come in
Eat, drink and be merry, don't think about sin.

Consider the difference when share prices fall
The stock market's dodgy, we might lose it all
and investing our trust and our all in the one -
who lay in the cradle, where the brightest star shone

He was Eternal and human, God head and man
Bringing salvation, all part of God's plan
As baby we love him, and celebrate well
But what about Easter, and heaven and hell?

Consider the difference between gaining and losing
and living for now, and deliberately choosing
To put Jesus first, and follow his ways
without him as our leader, life's just one big maze.

*Margaret Cockbain*

# IF I

If I surrender to Christ as my King,
If I let Him have everything.
If I give to The Master all of my days,
If I let Him have all of my praise,

If I work for Him every day,
If I point out to souls that 'this is the way'.
If I take Jesus Christ as my friend,
If I mean what I say and not just pretend,

If I serve Him forever by lip and by life,
If I trust Him to lead me through trouble and strife
If I were asked 'If I truly believe,'
'If I trust in the Lord, Life Eternal receive'

If I then go to seek for the lost,
If I show them His love regardless of cost,
If I am used each day for the Lord,
If I am used to send forth His Word,

If I look to the future in order to see,
If I have become what He wants me to be,
If I with His help may be able to learn,
If I His Holy will may discern.

If I am determined to follow the Lord,
If I am encouraged to dwell on His Word,
If I by faith can see everything clear,
If I can He'll help me all through the year,
If I can you can.

*SNIKPOHD*

# AT THE GATES

Standing perplexed at the gates of the temple
Bones weary: mind empty of all earthly thought
The sudden dawn of realisation makes me tremble
Has the moment arrived for the last battle to be fought?

Coil your loving arms round this fast decaying body
Let your eternal tenderness embrace me so
Though the heady fragrance linger of a lifetime full of memory
The time has finally come for letting go.

The faceless coachman bids me to enter his carriage
'But there is still so much here I have to do'
Yet time knows no mercy, no strength of courage
With great reluctance, I take my eternal leave of you.

Once inside the gloomy coach my earthly fears melt
The pains, the sorrows of a life once so hard
Are no longer known, no longer felt
My reckless soul has finally found peace in the Kingdom of God!

*Rosemaria Lucas-Foster*


# GATESHEAD ANGEL

I saw you being built,
Your strong structure,
Reflects skill and design,
You bring mixed feelings of Art,
But I think you are a beautiful
Sculpture of God's love,
Guiding and protecting us,
Into the future.

*Kenneth Mood*

## SERENITY

Oh, why can't we all have love and serenity
As we look all around us at everything God has made,
All abiding in peace and harmony with no outward signs of enmity
But beneath it all is a simmering pot of hatred, malice and ill-got trade.
We have but a short time on this earth,
So why do we spend it giving each other such a wide berth
When a smile and cheer plus a whole lot of love
Could turn us into that peaceful white dove?
So let's not waste a precious moment of our day
But open up our heart and say
Let peace be with you all
Then really we will all be 10 feet tall.

*Jean Rendell*


## WHO?

Who created Adam? Who created Eve?
Why do some have a faith while others don't believe?
Who created Adam and said he should be man?
Why not a bear, or tiger? A lion or a ram?
Who created Eve to take the apple from the tree?
To bring about disasters in the world for you and me?
Who said the earth should not be flat? Instead it should be round?
Who said that it would be through ears that we would then hear sound?
Who said that some would live in heat, and some would live in cold?
Who said when we were born we're young - and when we die we're
old?
Who said that some would be born black - and others would be white?
Who said that some should be blind - some have the gift of sight?
Who created Adam? Who created Eve?
Unlike most I have no faith - but wish I could believe!

*Letitia Snow*

## FOR A HAPPY LIFE

Live each day as if it's your last,
Look forward to the future and not to the past.
Believe in Jesus and follow our Saviour,
Ask His forgiveness and watch your behaviour.
Keep sight of your faith and keep it strong,
Love one another and know right from wrong.
Give the Lord your thanks and sing His praises,
Read of eternal life among the biblical phrases.
Rejoice in the fellowship of other Christians,
Make God proud when you're on His missions.
Remember God's love and what He's done,
For He gave the world His only Son.
So put your hands together and give thanks to the Lord,
For His comfort and strength and His loving word.
'We thank you Lord for all you've done,
The Cross of Calvary was the victory won.'

*Lorraine Dixon*


## BE STILL

What is this thing that we call life
Full of fun sadness trouble and strife,
But what is life without our Lord
Not knowing where to go, who to turn to.
Take a time during the day
Listen deep, you'll find what to say,
Be still, be quiet He'll be there
Your problems are His so let Him share
In all your thoughts, good or bad,
He is the best friend you'll ever have
Save your space a piece of day
A piece of time for you to pray.
Be still and know God.

*Don Friar*

## THE LITTLE ONES

'Unless you are like children'
Our good Lord once decreed
'You cannot enter Heaven's Gate,
Or on His Manna feed.'
This message was so simple
Yet somehow so profound,
For, when we see these little ones,
We are on solid ground.
Their trust and honesty is plain
For everyone to see,
Their disregard of race or creed
A joy for you and me.
So, when we grown-ups look around
At all this wide world's hate,
Let's grasp those little outstretched hands
Before it is too late.

*Joan Leahy*


## CHRISTIANITY TODAY

Where is Jesus in the church
Have we left him in the lurch
Empty pews and soulless voices
A carpenter's son has no choices.
If he came in today, long hair, a beard, no
                          money to pay.
The door would be closed, we'd turn him away.
Human nature doesn't change.
The odd and different we call strange.
And Jesus had a single mother
The kind of woman, about no-one would bother.
The government would stop her pay
And force her on to the streets to pray.

*Lucille Ercan*

## CONFLICT
*(From 'Reflections on Coriano Ridge'*
*- a war cemetery)*

Did they not run towards the foe
Down these twisting lanes, now new with tarmac?
Did they not search the horizon
For tell-tale smoke of tank exhausts?

Was it here they dived for cover
As the shell-fire sought them out?
Was it over quickly for them -
Young lives harshly terminated?

Did their anger leap before them
As they saw their comrades fall?
Did they charge, or did they scatter
Cowering from the steely hail?

Were there anguished cries of 'Father!'
Reaching out to God of youth?
Were there bitter screams in dying,
Sobbing out 'Why us? Why me?'

How were many acts of bravery
Done within the facts of war?
How was there splendid heroism
In face of hateful cruelty?

Were there tears among their comrades?
Stretcher-bearers breaking down
When they gathered death's sad harvest
From Coriano's rolling hills?

Above all the useless questions
Conviction's strident herald calls -
'It was cruel, it was bloody, but
My friend - it was for you!'

*Jo Allen*

## THE CARPENTER

Born of humble birth,
Lived His time as Man on earth.
But in His short allotted span,
He became Son of man,
He worked at a carpenter's bench,
And His thirst of knowledge, one could never quench,
When at the Temple His parents did stay,
From His followers, He would never sway,
His Disciples were without status or rank,
From common waters they all drank,
For fishermen were of His choice,
They followed Him, their hearts did rejoice,
He healed the sick, and clothed the poor,
Transporting His unfailing lore,
By gentleness and kindly deed,
His flock of sheep, he did feed,
Then, when triumphant into Jerusalem He rode,
So near now to His final abode,
They cheered and shouted, gave their acclaim,
Shouted out His glorious Name
But all too soon, the table was to turn,
Hearts once aglow, were soon to burn.
So soon to be nailed to a cross of wood,
Yet no one cared, few understood,
He lay there in His agony,
He did this for you, He did this for me
And whosoever rejects His Holy name,
So quenches that sacred flame,
Which inspires every living breath,
And in dying, gives life to death.

*B L Trelease*

# THE MESSAGE

Mary looked at the sheet of paper in front of her. It fascinated her to think that you could take a clean sheet of paper and, by adding symbols - letters, words - you could send a message. But today she had no message in her.

Idly she picked up a letter lying on the desk. It was from an old friend who had written, out of the blue, recounting all her family news. There was quite a bit of it as the two women had not met for several years. 'I just felt I had to write to you. Take care of yourself. Love as always, Sue.' And there, at the end, was a bible reference, as yet unread. It was typical of Sue to do such a thing - she had always been a committed Christian - but it was going to be strange for Mary to pick up her bible after so long. Well, inspiration was still missing, she would look up the verse - after she had hunted for her bible of course!

Eventually, there it was - Isaiah 43: verse 1 'Fear not, for I have redeemed you; I have called you by name, you are Mine.' The words sent a stab into her heart. For a while she could not move. It was so unexpected, so overwhelming. That had been the verse that had brought her to Christ; that had been the verse that had lead her to think about mission and the needs of others - so many light years earlier. What had happened? What had changed things? Her career mainly, and worldly friends, and a liking for expensive clothes, good holidays. Bu also something else. Fear. She still remembered the feeling of panic at the thought of an unknown lifestyle. And now here was God saying 'Fear not.' How come she had not noticed that before? No wonder she could not find a message to write. She needed to hear one first.

Slowly she got to her feet and went over to the phone. 'Sue, can we meet up sometime. I'd like to talk.'

*Pamela Fallas*

## HE WAS NOT THERE

Mary came to the garden tomb
In the silvery light of dawn,
With fragrant ointments and sweet perfume
She came in the early morn.
Her Saviour's body she sought with care -
But the tomb was empty, He was not there -
He was not there.

She stooped again to look inside
The cave where Jesus had been,
And saw an angel seated there -
And wondered what it could mean . . .
Her Saviour's grave-clothes were folded with care -
But the tomb was empty, He was not there -
He was not there.

She stood there weeping, then all at once
A voice behind her said:
'Who are you looking for in this place
Where the living bury their dead?'
'Sir, if you've taken Him, show me where,
For I've looked in the tomb, but He is not there -
He is not there.'

Then - 'Mary' He said in a voice that she knew,
And she fell at His feet and said
'My Master lives!' and her heart leapt for joy
That her Saviour was not dead:
He had conquered death, for she met Him where
The tomb was empty, He was not there -
He was not there.

*Joan Moore*

## GOD'S MIGHTIER

We can see the highest mountains,
We can see the mighty sea,
We look up to the heavens
There sun and moon we see.
We marvel at the twinkling stars,
The snowflakes thrill our soul
And over, under, all around the living God
Who's mightier than them all.

Man's climbed those highest mountains,
He's sailed the mighty seas.
He's flown up to the heavens
And marvelled there to see
How tiny is this universe that's home to you
and me.
With all man's mighty intellect, his powers
and his skills,
He cannot make a star to shine or hold a
snowflake still.
It takes a mightier power these wonders to perform,
Our living God is in control, and he's mightier than all.

*Nessie Shaw*


## PEACE IN THE ISLES

Peace could mean a bit of you and I and all of us,
So why can't we all sit down and talk without the fuss?
Let's hold hands together in friendship
And endeavour on a lasting relationship.

As this Good Friday dawns now,
Violence and hate must end but the question is how?
Innocent lives have been lost with no regret
From those who felt their cause was one of neglect.

Now as the day lingers on we pray
That all those around the table may have their say,
Ask the questions, find some answers and try to reconcile
And find the final peace that passeth all understanding with
a smile.

The day has come at last in a peaceful settlement
For one and all to accept each other's feelings is a miracle sent.
Remember all those who died and suffered but not in vain,
For you and I and all who love and care will be our glorious gain.

*Beryl Sylvia Rusmanis*

## CLASS OF LIFE

When *Jesus* carried the *cross,* he was showing man
the weight of the *Cross of Life.*
When he was nailed to the *cross,* he was showing us
man's inhumanity to man.
When he *died* on the *cross,* he was showing man how
*wrong* he could be.
But let us use this as *learning!*
Let us take the *cross* into our life,
For it will be our *crutch* when we are crippled by *life*
It will be a *star* showing us the way when we are *lost*
If we hold the *cross* in our hand it becomes a *sword*
Offering strength when we are weak.
Turn that *sword* to show the blade and you have a weapon
of *God* which is knowledge
Turn that sword to shine in the *dark* and you have a
*shield* against *evil*
Place the sword before you and you have a barrier against
all harmful thoughts.
I ask you *now* to accept the challenge *God* is offering
*Pick up the sword and be a crusader of truth*
In the name of the *Father, Son, and Holy Spirit.*

*Irene Catney*

## LIGHTNING STRIKE

Tap - tap - tap. I walk blindly down a road.
Tap - tap- tap. I am a blind man.
I tap my way through life.
Tap - tap - tap goes my metallic stick.
I find my way passed hidden obstacles,
I walk in a thick mist.
Drip - drip - drip. Rain begins to fall,
I pull up my collar against the wet assailant.
Thunder rolls in the distance. The rain is heavy now.
It runs down my neck, it wets my forehead.
People are rushing, people are running.
Pushing, shoving, running and shoving.
*Bang* - there is an explosion in my head.
A tremendous surge of power is coursing through my body.
My God! I've been struck by lightning.
Miracle of miracles, I can see! - I can see!
I behold the world and it is beautiful. Faces surround me.
Beautiful faces with beautiful eyes.
Thank you God, thank you for the gift of sight.
I can see! - I can see! A mighty power has restored it.
Just like Jesus restored the sight of the blind man.
Just as he restored the paralytic to full health.
Just as St Paul was struck by lightning and shown
The Truth of God in Jesus Christ.
Just as he restores us even now to a wholeness of life,
To be lived in the power and love of his Holy Spirit.

*Robert E Ford*

## THE LAST CALL

The call of death comes to us all,
The king, the peasant, great and small.
He comes in guise of different shades,
Some die quickly, some just fade.
To some it is an anguish great,
And for them there's no escape.
They see but nought beyond the grave,
They cry but there is none to save.
For they rejected God's dear Son,
Who on the cross a victory won.
And died that death should hold no fear
For those who hold His name so dear.
For those to whom His love's revealed
Are with the Holy Spirit sealed,
Unto salvation while on earth,
For they've experienced new birth.
It's not of earthly things we speak,
But of the heavenly things so deep.
For God, in Jesus lived and died
That in His love we might abide.
So when the time of death draws near.
We have no cause to fret or fear.
For when at last we cross the river,
The Lord who is the greatest giver,
Will to us give eternal life,
And rest from all our earthly strife,
To live with Him no more to roam
Content to dwell in Heaven's bright home.

*Andrea Macrow*

## WE WERE THERE

Yes Lord that was us, we were there.
Standing there at your cross,
Jeering, laughing and dancing with glee.
What fun, what bliss said we.

       Crucify. Crucify.

We did not know or care, it was your love for us
You were suffering and dying there.
You died that we might live forever
You died to free us all from sin.
You died to give us freedom of choice
To go down Satan's path
Or live with you in Paradise.
You love us so, you want us all
to be saved.
We only have to give our hearts to you
and ask you to come into our life.
You will walk with us through all
our strife
Until the day you come to take your place
and we will see you face to face.

Lord, we are sorry for our sins
We are sorry we danced with glee
       at Calvary.

*Ena Stanmore*

## OUR LORD'S COMING

I came to a stable cold and bare
And dark-eyed creatures came to stare
By simple folk news of my birth was spread -
Shepherds who knelt at my manger bed.

I came again when years had flown
To look for some to call my own,
I found them, simple fisher folk,
Who willingly followed and bore my yoke.

I came to the garden when they thought me dead,
With simple folk I broke my bread,
Then their eyes were opened and they knew their Lord,
For the rest of their lives spread the news abroad.

And still I come when prayers are said,
To simple hearts at the breaking of bread,
And with simple folk I'll still abide
Till Heaven and Earth are cast aside.

And then again for all to see,
I'll come in splendid majesty
And lead to a bright new heaven above,
Those simple folk who gave me their love.

*Irene Wallace*

## FREEDOM - MARTYRDOM

None less than freedom
Gained from some blood
Blood from the body of chapel
A chapel filled with your love

I don't know why I did not see this before
Your heart has set me free, there is darkness no more

And your name is Jesus, a name above names
A name that set me free

Now that you are here, there is nothing to fear
I wasn't to know that I live by what I swear
You have given me heart, a new start
Hope to keep on, but no one hears my harp.

Meaningless thing called life, I hope to be
More than lost, less than free
A slave to wisdom, let that be my way
The sands of time washed away,
I am the rock that stayed.

And now I am happy
The Lord has given me purpose
It's up to us now, I must claim what's rightfully mine.

*Koye Oyedeji*

## COLOUR-BLIND

Of all the colours in this world,
Our Father made them all.
Each little flower that opens,
Each tree short or tall.
The blue of the sky above,
And even sometimes grey,
When out of its very depth,
A storm is on its way.

Then the golden sun does shine,
To show the way is clear,
For the rainbow in the sky
Will surely now appear
With colours there for all to see.

The yellow black, of the bumble bee,
Pink blossom of a flowering tree,
Many colours created He.

The minds of man - us His creation,
Is colour there within.
Creeds and colour make a Nation.
And when many look around
The colour of their mind is dim.

*For they see*

The different nationalities,
And the colour of their skin.
But others then will look around,
Their mind colour and light,
For they see what the Father meant,
That we should mix and be content.

God mixed the colours of mankind,
For God is love and colour-blind.

**Shirley K Monaco**

## WHITSUN COMFORT

When I am lonely, God is near,
And if I listen, I can hear
His Comforter who speaks to me
A message, O my God, from Thee.

If life be stormy, God is still,
If I but cleave to His true will,
An anchor I may call on thrice
Unto the shore of paradise.

If I am sad, God lifts my heart
To where He can pure joy impart
Above the aether's sapphire rim,
Where light and glee grow never dim.

When problems shower upon my head
And thunderclouds their rains have shed,
My God is waiting for me still
To guide me gently to His will.

When friends and loved ones all desert
Me, loneliness and death just hurt
Me, then God's love like spring-bright sun
To me as Comforter doth run.

When I am lonely, God will come,
The Comforter who is not dumb,
Who comfortable words will speak
To all who for Him truly seek.

*Martin Burr*

# IT'S NOT TOO LATE!

Reach out for help -
*It's not too late!*
Don't give in to doom
Or personal self-hate.
Believe and accept
Jesus' forgiveness of your wrong doings,
He can take away
Your stale, self-doubting; mind brewings.
We are all of
*God's* invention,
Not robots
Held in mind-numbed suspension.
We are free
To accept Him - or not.
But Hell . . .
Is a nasty place to rot.
We can do what's wrong;
Stoking Hell's fires -
And in its flames
Our salvation expires . . .
Heaven isn't just made up
From our imagination -
Accepting Jesus means
*Everlasting life and salvation.*

**Sheryl Williamson**

## OUR PRAYER

How often do we pray to God
When things start going wrong
We ask of Him so many things
As we go along
Prayer is a wonderful contact
And deep inside of me
I know He will answer in His way
For I believe in Him you see
When prayer means what we say
We get the feeling of love
Which really we know inside of us
Comes from God above.
So bow your heads in prayer
Any place, anywhere
For God is there to listen
And give you every care.

*Mary Campbell-Bridgman*


## THE INCANDESCENT CROSS

See how the grasses
bow when He passes.
See when He smiles,
along the church aisles,
that the beam of light,
symbolically bright,
dwells fondly on the sign
of His Son's supreme fine
and the golden crucifixes,
set in holy niches,
glow proudly round those
hallowed chapel walls.

*Florence Frost*

## EXHILARATION

Joy like a lightning flash
Trembles through my being.
I drink in the clean new smell
Of dry earth after rain.

My quivering nostrils expand
At the fragrance of new wet grass,
I lift up my hands to the sky,
Into immensity I almost fly.

Then rushing down the hill
With the wind in my hair,
Boundless joy, limitless love,
Fill my soul, expand my heart.

Such ecstasy, I know only You can give,
Yearning I reach out for You,
Touch me, Lord, touch me,
I know, I know, You are here.

*Marie Jay*


## I SPY

Spiders hang over us as in bed we lie.
Suspended there to catch a fly
if some spot it they let out a scream
others just smile and stay serene
different human beings, different ways
come from our make-up in childhood days
everybody on this earth today all
have something else to say but
those who know God are one step ahead
for these the spider never touches the bed.

*Valvy Hope*

## LOST IN JESUS

I'm lost in You Jesus, my Saviour, my passion -
Yes, whether or not You are this season's fashion.
You've welcomed me in and You've saved me by grace,
And now up in heaven You've kept me a place.
It's You that I love and it's You I adore -
Please pour out Your love and Your Spirit some more.
Consume all my longing, consume all my thirst,
And in all that I do I will honour You first.
Without You in my life, Jesus, I can do nought,
And yet with Your precious blood I have been bought.
Your love's like a magnet -so awesome in power -
Stay close by my side every day and each hour.
For never before have I found such a treasure -
Your love, joy and peace just spill out in full measure.
But how can I say thanks for loving me so -
And searching me out when You could have let go.
For You are all loving - You held me for years,
And You journeyed along with my smiles and my tears.
I'm lost in Your love, and I'll n'er be the same.
You know all about me, including my name.
Now my life is so changed in my habits and style;
For You have enriched it and made it worthwhile.
How can I repay all the pain You went through -
For You died for my sins and You washed me anew.
Your love is so precious, it's sweet and divine:
And now I am Yours and forever You're mine.
For I have been saved - I'm a child of the King,
I'll love You forever: I'll worship and sing.
And like a kind shepherd You care and You lead,
You fill up my being; You're all that I need.

*Susan Kendall*

## GOD'S SIGNATURE

Listen!
You can hear the wind rustle in the leaves,
The sound of the rain,
Gently restoring, washing the earth's plains.
Look!
You can see the sunlight,
Rainbow colours glinting, shining through the clouds.
Feel!
The wind caress your face,
The sun warm your heart.

Fall of the night -
Sunrise -
Sunset -

The depth of the sea,
The glory of the skies,
The green of the leaves,
The Autumn barren-ness
Waiting to be renewed - reborn,
Yet rich in hues of gold and brown.

Colours - colours of nature,
Nature in all its glory,
In abundance.

Truly this is God,
God's signature upon the world.

*Helena Abrahams*

## THE EUCHARIST

There is no hunger that cannot be fed,
No thirst that nothing in the world can slake:
For every longing, so the wise have said,
Must be some ease the weary soul may take.

Thus appetite is proof that there's relief
Of appetite: it cannot be we burn
For what is not. So, too, our sure belief
That God must be, because for God we yearn.

But we are mortal still: our senses burst
For loving arms to bind us breathless tight,
Soft beds for sleep, deep rivers when we thirst,
For touch and taste, for scent and sound and sight.

O' God, who made all hungers, give us meat.
'This is my body, child. Take and eat.'

*Paul Chown*


## A MESSAGE I REMEMBER

Before I left heaven, before my own birth,
God gave me advice for my journey on earth.
He said you are me, a magnificent being,
But I give you free will and a choice of your seeing.
Go forth and create, inspire and enjoy,
What form shall I give you, a girl or a boy.
Whatever you're thinking, for you what is true,
To the very last detail, will happen to you.
One word of caution, before you depart,
If ever you need me, just look to your heart.
Now that you're ready, I'll blow you to earth,
The mother you chose, is ready for birth.

*André Smith*

## ALPINE MUSIC

Tiptoeing gently, laughing, dancing -
Skipping, jumping, whirling, prancing
Silver flecks glistening in sunlight swirling
Twisting in shallows; whispering, gurgling.
Gliding melodiously as waters deepen;
Side-stepping smooth stones, by time made even.
So flows the stream with its ageless song!
Come join the dance, come dance along!

Leaves rustle together, wind whispering through branches;
Emerald and lime-green, patterned by sun's glances.
Climbing the mountain slopes with effortless grace,
Joining the dance with unhurried pace.
Higher and higher on tiptoe, trees rise -
Dance onward, dance upward
Stretch up to the skies!

High mountain peaks, majestic and towering,
Grand, glorious they stand with arms spread, empowering.
White teethed, open-mouthed with deep thundering voice
Their song joins nature's dance -
Rejoice, rejoice!

Birds add to the chorus as catching the breeze
They dart upward and hover with well controlled ease.
Full throated their melody blends with the singing
Paeans of praise - the whole air seems ringing!
Dance, sing they cry, come dance and sing -
Come join with us, praise creation's King!

*C E McBain*

# THE GIFT

The coming of the Holy Spirit
Promise of Jesus fulfilled,
With one accord they received it
Their very beings, were thrilled
Twas the parting gift, of Jesus
To his faithful followers few
So, on keeping this holy tryst
There were many, believed true.

The sounds of a mighty rushing wind
Flames, and tongues of fire
Touched, each one gathered there
And all, desired souls to win
From, that upper room they came
Filled with imparted light
Three thousand souls that day were won!
The work of the Holy Spirit had
Begun

*Charlotte Bryon Armstrong*

# AN EASTER PICTURE

Picture the cross on Calvary's hill,
The Man of God obeying God's will,
Hanging there for all to see
This is the way of eternity.

Picture the dark clouds looming above,
The Man of God displaying his love,
In his own body bearing our pain
The eternal Lamb of God was slain.

Picture him now in the murky grave,
Conquering death our souls to save,
Death has no hold on Our Lord this day
As now he rolls the stone away.

Picture the hope of his resurrection,
Bringing us joy, peace and direction,
Follow him now and act in his name
This is the gospel we proclaim.

*Irene Harrow*

## KEEPING FAITH

So many years of heartache
So many years of pain
I often wondered how I coped
Could I do it all again?

I must admit I lost my faith
Thinking no one cared
Was there anybody up there
Did no one hear my prayer?

Tears that I kept hidden
When hopes were very low
Feelings that I can't explain
That no one else will know

But I know now that I was chosen
For a special task
Someone did believe in me . . .
                        *Maybe* I didn't *ask* . . .

*Gwen Tominey*

## THE PROMISE OF MORNING

There was no light in the room. The curtains were open but the cloud-filled night was dismally black. No moon, no stars. Drawing the curtains would have made no difference to the darkness inside or out. This was the cold dark of the December night. a slight wind chilled through and occasionally surprised with a gust, shaking and rattling ill-fitting doors and windows. Despite the darkness it was not late, barely seven o'clock, yet the stillness was complete. Beyond the rattling window there was no sound.

A fire in a grate, a figure dozing in an armchair, female form, blanket across her legs. She was so used, now, to sitting here in this chair, her darkness surrounding, that she lost track of whether she was asleep or awake. She thought she recalled or dreamt a visitor. A stranger, yet she had told him more than she had ever told anyone, about her blindness, her anger, her adoption, her bitterness towards her parents, her unkindness towards her aunt, her fear of the doctors, her abandonment of hope and finally this - her existence in a dark room, cold despite the glowing fire and the day after day tiredness and pointlessness of it all. And yet with this visitor she had felt comfortable, an unusual and unexplained sensation for her.

But then he had asked to touch her eyes. No-one touched her. The memories of countless doctors, nurses, specialists, prodding, probing, peering, and ultimately failing, had made her determined that no-one would ever touch her again. He had harshly told her that she would not see if she did not believe it possible and she had angrily told him to leave her alone and it was in the silence following her outburst that she had eventually fallen asleep. And now, the calmness returned, a thought came to her.

'I know who you are' she said.

'Good.' was his reply.

'And I believe I will see.'

'Good.'

She felt the dampness of his touch on her eyes and soon fell into a
beautiful dream of colours and faces and light and the promise of
morning.

*John Daly*


## UNTITLED

When I need someone you're always there
I close my eyes and say a prayer
You walk with me through good times and bad
You're with me whether I'm happy or sad

You give me strength to face each day
Comfort me and show the way
When sorrow is too much to bear
I turn to you and know you care

You're in the wind and spring showers
In the rustle of trees, the smell of flowers
You're in the beauty we touch and see
But best of all God, you walk with me

*Sylvia Austin*

## UNCONDITIONAL LOVE

This is my life, my little life, I bring it to you.
Carrying it in open hand to give it to you as a gift.
It comes gift-wrapped for it is precious,
as precious as the day when you first gave it to me many years ago.

As a small child I am eager for you to untie the bow and take off
the wrapping paper - I so want you to be delighted with my little gift.

Your eyes meet mine, and with great tenderness you take my parcel,
holding it carefully, and together we share a moment of stillness,
busy with expectation.

Oh so gently your fingers move across the paper to the bow and
in that moment of release the paper falls aside and I see -
not the present I have wrapped, but what, in your hands I have become.

I recognise the pain, the hurt, the sadness, I see the strivings,
failure, tiredness and disease, and almost as shadows the joy,
the peace, the excitement of you at work in, and through my life.

For one heart stopping moment I fear you will say
'Is that all there is?' - instead you take me in your arms,
holding me close, wanting me as I want you -
Lover desiring as much to be with the Beloved
as she desires to be with Him.

*Pam Ritchie*

# GUIDING LIGHT
*(Written for my dear friend Valli Luschwitz, on her 70th birthday)*

When darkness falls - in sad times
And problems are around,
I take my thoughts to Jesus
Where comfort can be found.

Before I focus on His love
I know she helps me there,
The warmth and strength she sends me
No other can compare.

Encouragement beholds me
Through her the link is made,
My prayers and hers unite in force
As fear begins to fade.

I know my thoughts are being heard
I have no doubts to tell,
With guidance from her special love
I understand so well.

Dear Valli, it's of you I speak
And for all the work you do,
For all your kindness - in all your ways
God shines his light through you . . .

***Lena McGrath***

## THE LORD IS NEAR

When you feel down in the dumps
And nothing's going right for you
There's a friend who can help
And nothing's too difficult
For him to do

This friend is called Jesus
Who knows our frailty
He knows everything we go through
And what we want to be

He hears our cry for help
When we've come to the end of the rope
And only gives us what
We are able to handle
So through it we can cope

He wants what's best for us
Although we can't see it at the time
When we should be looking forward
We tend to look behind

So when one door shuts
Another one will open
He will give you the key to turn it
And who knows what will happen

*Jeannie H*

# GRIEF

*(Dedicated to the family of Lucille Morrison nee Rowley,*
*in her memory 'A Friend')*

Aftermath,
visiting that place of bittersweet memories, is fleeting and hazy.
Unable as yet, to partake of all that was our loved one,
the erupting pain, coming when least expected, seems at
times almost too intense to bare.

Time limps on, our visits to our cherished memories,
more frequent, and less fleeting,
separation of pain, and our memories,
enables us to stay and visit a little
longer each time now.

More time passes, pain and memories,
manageable,
permitting us so to reacquaint ourselves,
with the delight of our loved one was to us,
and still is . . .

Time they say heals. No such thing, it is God that heals,
it is God whom holds our loved ones in his keeping.
It is Jesus that has made the bridge between life and death,
and we can be assured, of His Love, Peace and Presence, during this,
our
dark time,
and forever
more.

***Glynes Mewton***

## FRIENDS

Everybody needs a friend
To help them on their way
With maybe just a phone call
To check that they're OK
A simple word of greeting
To a stranger passing by,
A nod, a smile, a cheerful wave
Can lift their spirits high
If you're feeling rather lonesome
Or someone's let you down
Remember, that a happy face
Looks better than a frown.
You won't encourage others
If you look forever blue
So always try to wear a smile
it's a simple thing to do.
When you wake up in the morning
Make a promise, that, today,
You're going to help somebody
And guide them on their way.
If you keep that smile upon you face
In almost everything you do
You'll find that all the folk you meet
Will feel much brighter too.

*A D Tarbox*

# INFORMATION

We hope you have enjoyed reading this book - and that you will continue to enjoy it in the coming years.

If you like reading and writing poetry drop us a line, or give us a call, and we'll send you a free information pack.

Write to :-
**Triumph House Information**
**1-2 Wainman Road**
**Woodston**
**Peterborough**
**PE2 7BU**
**(01733) 230749**

L12
4PV